High-Wing Aircraft
Visualized Flight Maneuvers Manual **Fifth Edition**

For Pilots in Training

AVIATION SUPPLIES & ACADEMICS, INC.
NEWCASTLE, WASHINGTON

High-Wing Aircraft
Visualized Flight Maneuvers Manual
Fifth Edition

Aviation Supplies & Academics, Inc.
7005 132nd Place SE
Newcastle, Washington 98059
asa@asa2fly.com | 425-235-1500 | asa2fly.com

ASA-VFM-HI-5
ISBN 978-1-64425-223-9

Additional format available:
eBook PDF ISBN 978-1-64425-224-6

Printed in the United States of America

2026   2025   2024   2023   9   8   7   6   5   4   3

Cover photo: iStock.com/mikvivi

[03]

PREFACE

The purpose of this handbook is threefold:

1. To provide the student with a more thorough understanding of the basic parts of each flight maneuver, in order to better prepare them for each flight instruction period;
2. To provide a foundation for later formal training for private, commercial, or flight instructor candidates;
3. To create a safer and more competent pilot.

This book should be used as a supplement to the current FAA Certification Standards for the certificate being sought. For a full discussion of each maneuver, refer to the *Airplane Flying Handbook* (FAA-H-8083-3). Airplane manufacturer recommendations should be checked before beginning any maneuver.

Maneuvers required by the FAA Certification Standards for the Sport, Private, Commercial, and Flight Instructor certificates are illustrated in this book. The minimum requirements established in the FAA Certification Standards for each certificate accompany each maneuver. Flight Instructor applicants are required to meet the Commercial Pilot skill level. For those maneuvers that are Private Pilot-only, the Flight Instructor applicant is expected to perform the maneuvers more precisely than a Private Pilot applicant, as determined by the examiner.

Where it is appropriate, space has been provided for you to enter the tire pressures, tank capacities, airspeeds, power settings, etc. that apply to the airplane being flown.

Before practicing each maneuver, remember to complete the necessary preparations. Memory aid: **AAACT** ("act")

Area	terrain appropriate for maneuvering, and emergency landing area available
Airspeed	maneuvering speed (V_A) or as designated by practical test standards
Altitude	as designated by practical test standards
Clearing turns	clear area for traffic
Technique	as designated by FAA Certification Standards

The maneuvers are visual, and require you to keep your center of attention outside the aircraft. When practicing the maneuvers, use outside references to perform the maneuver, then cross-check by scanning the instruments inside the cockpit—look outside, peek inside.

CONTENTS

AIRCRAFT REVIEW

Aircraft Model and Type:

_____

1. What is the normal climb-out speed? _____
2. What is the best rate-of-climb speed (V_Y)? _____
3. What is the best angle-of-climb speed (V_X)? _____
4. What is the maximum flaps-down speed (V_{FE})?_____
5. What is the maximum gear-down speed (V_{LE})?_____
6. What is the stall speed in a normal landing configuration (V_{S0})? _____
7. What is the clean (flaps and gear up) stall speed (V_{S1})? _____
8. What is the approach-to-landing speed? _____
9. What is the maneuvering speed (V_A)? _____
10. What is the never-exceed speed (V_{NE})? _____
11. What is the maximum structural cruising speed (V_{NO})? _____
12. What engine-out glide speed will give you the maximum range? _____
13. What airspeed is used for a
    Short-field takeoff? _____ Short-field landing? _____
    Soft-field takeoff? _____ Soft-field landing? _____
14. What is the service ceiling? _____
15. What is the make and horsepower of the engine?
    _____
16. What is the estimated true airspeed at 5,000 feet and 65% power? _____
17. What RPM or combination of RPM and manifold pressure yields 65% power at 5,000 feet MSL?
    _____ RPM _____ MP
18. How many gallons of fuel are consumed per hour at 65% power at 5,000 feet MSL? _____

Magnetic Compass

Flight Controls
Elevators

The elevators provide control of the pitch attitude about the airplane's lateral axis. Elevators are the key to controlling the angle of attack.

- When control wheel (yoke) is pulled toward pilot, the nose pitches up.

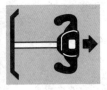 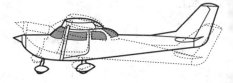

- When control wheel (yoke) is pushed away from pilot, the nose pitches down.

 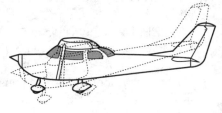

(continued)

Airspeed Indicator
Pitot-Static System

Altimeter
Static System

Vertical Speed Indicator
Static System

Turn Coordinator
Usually Electric

Attitude Indicator
Vacuum System

Heading Indicator
Vacuum System

19. How many usable gallons of fuel can your aircraft carry? _____

20. Where are the fuel tanks located and what are their capacities?

Main tank _____	gallons	_____
Left tank _____	gallons	_____
Right tank _____	gallons	_____
Rear tank _____	gallons	_____
Auxiliary tanks_____	gallons	_____

21. With full fuel, 65% power, at 5,000 feet, allowing a 45 minute reserve, what is the maximum duration (in hours)? _____

22. What speed will give you the best glide ratio? _____

23. What is the octane rating and color of the fuel used by the aircraft? _____

24. How do you drain the fuel sumps?
_____

25. What weight of oil is used? _____

26. Is the landing gear fixed, manual, hydraulic, or electric?_____ If retractable, what is the back-up system for lowering the gear? _____
_____

27. What is the maximum demonstrated allowable crosswind component for the aircraft? _____

28. How many persons will the aircraft safely carry with full fuel? _____

29. What is the maximum allowable weight the aircraft can carry in the baggage compartments? _____

30. What takeoff distance is required to clear a 50-foot obstacle at maximum gross weight at a pressure altitude of 5,000 feet and 90°F (assume no wind and a hard-surfaced runway)? _____

31. What would be the answer to Question 30 if the takeoff was made from sea level pressure altitude?
_____

32. Does high humidity increase or decrease the takeoff distance? _____

33. What landing distance is required at 2,300 pounds at a pressure altitude of 2,000 feet and standard temperature (assume no wind or obstacle)?

_____

34. How do you determine pressure altitude?

_____

35. What is your maximum allowable useful load?

_____

36. Solve the weight and balance problem for the flight plan you intend to fly. If you plan to fly solo, also solve the problem for a 180-pound passenger in each seat. Does your load fall within the weight and balance envelope?_____ What is your gross weight?_____ If you solved the problem with 180-pound passengers in each seat, how much fuel could you carry?_____ Where would this fuel be tanked?_____ If you carry full fuel, how much baggage could you carry?_____ Where would this baggage be placed? _____

V Speeds

V_A	Design maneuvering speed
V_F	Design flap speed
V_{FE}	Maximum flap extended speed
V_{LE}	Maximum landing gear extended speed
V_{LO}	Maximum landing gear operating speed
V_{NE}	Never-exceed speed
V_{NO}	Maximum structural cruising speed
V_{S0}	Stalling speed or the minimum steady flight speed in the landing configuration
V_{S1}	Stalling speed or the minimum steady flight speed obtained in a specific configuration
V_X	Best angle-of-climb speed
V_Y	Best rate-of-climb speed

AIRPLANE FAMILIARIZATION

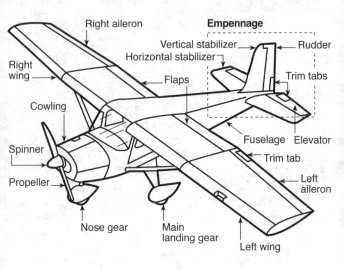

Empennage

Right aileron
Vertical stabilizer
Rudder
Horizontal stabilizer
Right wing
Flaps
Trim tabs
Cowling
Spinner
Fuselage
Elevator
Propeller
Trim tab
Left aileron
Nose gear
Main landing gear
Left wing

Flight Instruments

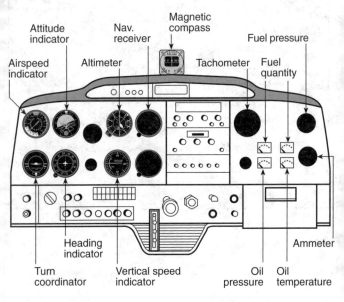

Attitude indicator
Nav. receiver
Magnetic compass
Fuel pressure
Airspeed indicator
Altimeter
Tachometer
Fuel quantity

Heading indicator
Ammeter
Turn coordinator
Vertical speed indicator
Oil pressure
Oil temperature

Ailerons

The primary use of the ailerons is to bank, or roll, the airplane around the longitudinal axis. Banking the wings results in the airplane turning in the direction of the bank.

- When control wheel (yoke) is turned to the left, left aileron is raised and airplane rolls to the left.

 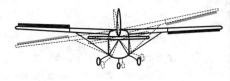

- When control wheel (yoke) is turned to the right, right aileron is raised and airplane rolls to the right.

 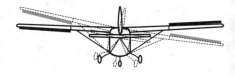

Rudder

The rudder is used to control the direction (left or right) of yaw about the airplane's vertical axis.

- When left rudder is pushed, the nose pivots to the left.

 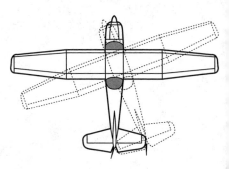

- Inspect right flap, on track, rod and hinges free
- Check right aileron for freedom of movement, hinges, counterweights, control linkage, security

- Check condition of right wing tip
- Check condition of right wing leading edge and bottom surface

4

- Remove right wing tie-down
- Check main wheel general condition and tire inflation
  Manufacturer Recommended tire inflation _____ psi
- Check brakes, hydraulic line, no leaks
- Check fuel condition through quick drain

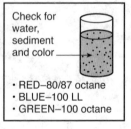

Check for water, sediment and color

- RED–80/87 octane
- BLUE–100 LL
- GREEN–100 octane

- Visually check fuel quantity and secure cap
  Tank capacity _____ gallons
- Inspect condition of wing top surface

(continued)

- Master switch ON
- Check fuel quantity
- Flaps down
- Turn aircraft lights on
- Visually check aircraft lights are operational and not damaged
- Turn aircraft lights off
- Master switch OFF
- Fuel selector on BOTH

- Inspect general condition of fuselage, empennage, horizontal stabilizer, and tail light
- Remove control surface lock
- Disconnect tail tie-down
- Check elevator for freedom of movement, cable condition, cotter pins

- Check rudder for freedom of movement, cable condition, cotter pins

- Inspect general condition of trim tab

- Inspect general condition of empennage and fuselage

- When right rudder is pushed, the nose pivots to the right.

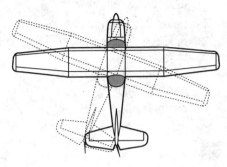

Cockpit Controls

Yoke

Hold yoke with your left hand. Your grip should be firm but relaxed.

Rudder pedals

Place your heels on the floor and toes, or the balls of the feet, on the rudder pedals. Pressures can be exerted more accurately by the toes, or the balls of the feet, than by the instep.

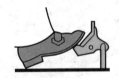

Brakes

To apply the airplane brakes, depress the top of the rudder pedals. Do the same when setting the parking brake.

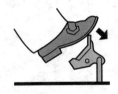

Throttle

Operate the throttle with the right hand. Hold the throttle so that small changes can be made smoothly. Use several fingers to act as a stop against contact with the panel or quadrant. Do not hold the throttle entirely by its knob or lever handle.

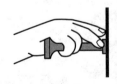

Flaps

Flaps increase the wing's lift by increasing its area or its camber. Flaps also cause drag because they extend beneath the wing. The lift/drag ratio is determined by the degree of flap extension. Using flaps lowers the wing's stalling speed, and increases the rate of descent without an increase in airspeed.

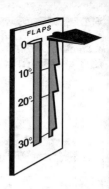

Trim Tab

The purpose of trim tab is to relieve control pressure on the flight controls. Set trim for airspeed (attitude) desired. The trim tab is operated by the trim wheel.

Forces Acting on the Airplane in Flight

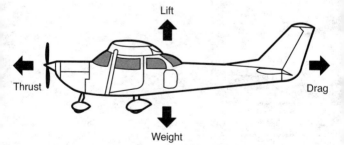

PREFLIGHT OPERATIONS

Check Manufacturer Recommendations

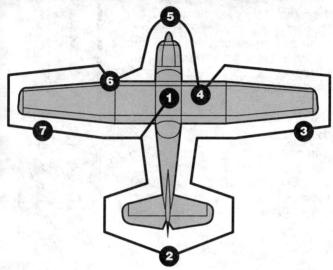

Upon approaching airplane:

- Perform visual check for general condition of aircraft
- Remove accumulations of frost, ice, or snow from wing
- Have flashlight available for night flight

- Check aircraft paperwork

Remember:

A irworthiness
R egistration
O wner's manual
W eight and balance
E quipment list

- Check pilot's paperwork, including valid pilot certificate and medical certificate
- Set parking brake
- Remove control wheel lock
- Ignition switch OFF
- Mixture idle cut-off

5

- Check oil level per manufacturer recommendations

- Fill oil for extended flight
- Make sure dipstick is properly seated
- Check cowl access door and inspect covers for security
- Check engine for signs of oil or fuel leaks
- Check ignition wires tight
- Check fittings and motor mount
- Drain fuel strainer in engine compartment, check for contaminants, water, color
- Check for bird or animal nests
- Check exhaust for tightness and cracks
- Check propeller and spinner for nicks, dents, cracks, and security
- Check alternator belt and attach bolts are tight and secure
- Check carburetor air filter and intake screen for foreign matter
- Check nose wheel strut clean and exposed at least 2 inches

- Check fuel quantity

- Check airspeed indicator—zero
- Check attitude indicator—erect and horizon adjusted
- Check altimeter—set barometric pressure or field elevation
- Check turn coordinator—during taxi
- Check heading indicator—during taxi, and set to magnetic compass or runway heading
- Check vertical speed indicator—zero
- Check flight controls are free and correct
- Mixture RICH (full in) below 3,000 feet density altitude, or lean to maximum RPM at full throttle at higher density altitudes
- Carburetor heat COLD (full in)
- Verify fuel selector on BOTH
- Set elevator trim for takeoff

- Set flaps for takeoff
- Aircraft lights ON
- Pitot heat as required
- Transponder on ALT
- Note time off

- Check oil pressure is in the green within 30 seconds
- Check starter disengaged (if starter were to remain engaged, ammeter would indicate full scale charge with engine running at 1,000 RPM)
- Lights ON as required
- Radios ON
- Flaps UP

BEFORE-TAKEOFF CHECK

Check Manufacturer Recommendations
- Complete preflight inspection (see Page 4)
- Complete starting airplane check (see Page 6)
- Position aircraft to avoid run-up over loose gravel or blasting other aircraft
- Set parking brake
- Check seats, seatbelts, shoulder harnesses secure

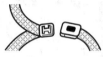

- Close and lock cabin doors and windows
- Throttle to 1,700 RPM
- Check both magnetos (RPM drop should not exceed 125 RPM on either magneto or 50 RPM differential between magnetos)
- Check carburetor heat for RPM drop
- Check engine instruments are in green arc
- Check ammeter is functioning properly
- Check suction gauge is in green arc
- Throttle to IDLE
- Set radios and avionics

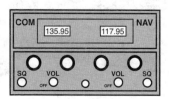

- Remove nose gear chock
- Check nose gear tire, cuts, bruise, inflation meet manufacturer recommendations
- Check nose gear actuating rods are straight
- Check windshield and cabin windows for cleanliness and no cracks
- Inspect static source on side of fuselage for blockage

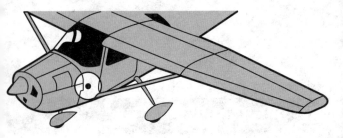

- Remove left wing tie-down
- Check main wheel general condition and tire inflation
  Manufacturer Recommended tire inflation _____ psi
- Check brakes, hydraulic line, no leaks
- Check fuel condition through quick drain
- Visually check fuel quantity and secure cap
  Tank capacity _____ gallons
- Inspect condition of wing top surface
- Check left wing leading edge and bottom surface
- Remove pitot tube cover
- Check pitot tube opening for blockage
- Check fuel tank vent opening for blockage
- Check stall warning vent opening for blockage and stall warning vane for freedom of movement

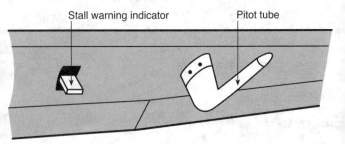

Stall warning indicator   Pitot tube

- Check condition of left wing tip
- Check left aileron for freedom of movement, hinges, counterweights, control linkage, security
- Inspect left flap, on track, rod and hinges free

General Checks:

- Check underbelly of airplane for excess oil and dirt
- Check baggage is secure and baggage compartment door is closed
- Check all windows are clean and free of cracks
- Inspect the airplane with reference to the checklist
- Verify the airplane is in safe flight condition

STARTING AIRPLANE

Check Manufacturer Recommendations

- Complete preflight inspection (see Page 4)
- Complete passenger briefing
- Adjust and lock seat, seatbelts, shoulder harnesses

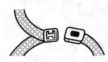

- Test and set brakes

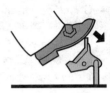

- Check circuit breakers in
- All electrical equipment off
- Fuel selector valve on BOTH
- Prime as required (2-6 strokes for cold engine, 0 strokes for warm engine)
- Lock primer
- Carburetor heat COLD (full in)

- Throttle OPEN 1/8 inch

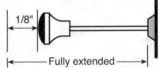

- Mixture RICH (full in) below 3,000 feet density altitude, or lean to maximum RPM at full throttle at higher density altitudes
- Clear propeller area, and call CLEAR PROP
- Master switch ON
- Ignition switch START (release when engine starts)

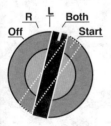

TAXIING

(Private, Sport, Commercial, CFI)

Objective: Safely maneuver the airplane on the ground.

Task:
- After engine start, align heading indicator with magnetic compass
- Obtain clearance to taxi
- Hold yoke to apply crosswind taxi corrections. Memory aid: Fly into, dive away

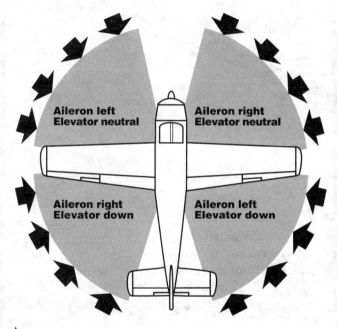

Aileron left
Elevator neutral

Aileron right
Elevator neutral

Aileron right
Elevator down

Aileron left
Elevator down

 Indicated Wind Direction Taxiing

- Rest heels on the floor

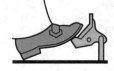

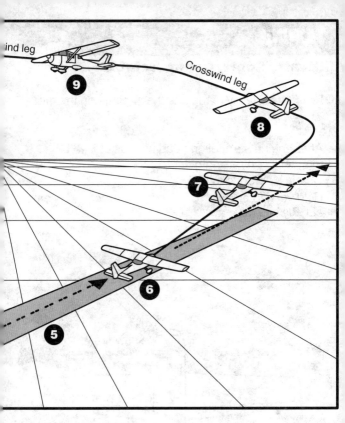

- Keep straight with rudder
- Keep wings level with aileron
- Check RPM for full power
- Check engine instruments are in the green arc
- Ease the weight off nose wheel as elevator becomes effective

(continued)

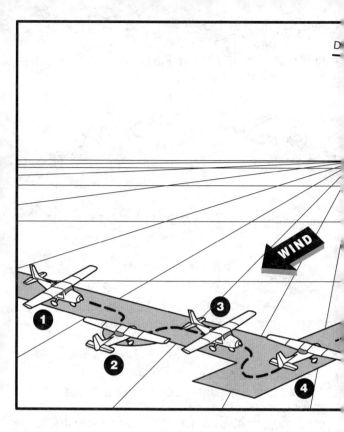

- Keep heels on floor, and toes on rudder pedals, not brakes

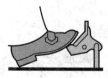

- Apply full throttle smoothly and positively

- Reduce power to IDLE
- Release parking brake
- Apply sufficient power with the throttle to start airplane moving forward

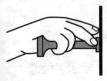

- Reduce power to idle and gently test brakes

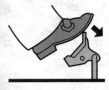

- Apply sufficient power to begin taxiing again
- Adjust power to maintain safe taxiing speed (a fast walking pace or less)
- More power may be required to start moving than is required to keep moving
- Steering is not possible until the airplane is rolling forward
- Control steering with the rudder pedals, and if necessary, differential braking
- While turning airplane, make sure the heading indicator rotates in the direction of turn (right turn increases numbers, left turn decreases numbers)

- While turning airplane, make sure the turn indicator deflects in the direction of the turn
- While turning airplane, make sure the coordination ball shows a skid in the opposite direction of the turn

Evaluation:

- Check brakes immediately after airplane begins moving
- When brakes are used, close throttle (do not use power against brakes)
- Use low power setting when taxiing, 1,000 RPM or less
- Position flight controls properly for existing wind conditions
- Extend courtesy to open hangars, buildings, people (when taxiing, debris, air, and noise is blown opposite the direction of travel)
- Keep speed under control at all times; no faster than would be safe without brakes (fast walking pace)
- Slow down before attempting turns
- Avoid sudden bursts of throttle and sharp braking, especially in strong quartering tailwinds
- Observe local taxi rules, ATC instructions, and airport markings
- Be alert for hazards such as ground obstructions, snow banks, gas pumps, ground vehicles, other aircraft (parked or moving)
- Practice situational awareness and runway incursion avoidance procedures
- Use a taxi chart during taxi
- Complete the appropriate checklist

NORMAL TAKEOFF & CLIMB

(Private, Sport, Commercial, CFI)

Objective: Takeoff and climb out to the downwind leg of the traffic pattern.

Task: Check Manufacturer Recommendations

- Complete preflight inspection (see Page 4)
- Complete starting airplane check (see Page 6)
- Taxi to the upwind runway

- Complete before-takeoff check (see Page 6)
- Wing flaps 0° for normal takeoff

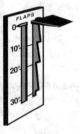

- Know local airport traffic pattern and altitude procedures
- Practice situational awareness and runway incursion avoidance procedures

- Obtain takeoff and departure clearances, if required
- Look out and check that runway and approaches are all clear

- Line up on runway centerline, nose wheel straight
- Select a reference point straight ahead for tracking

- Leave runway at lift-off speed

Manufacturer Recommended lift-off speed _____ knots
- Use right rudder to offset torque as required

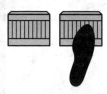

- Keep right hand on the throttle

7

- Establish the attitude that results in V_Y with full throttle
  Manufacturer Recommended V_Y _____ knots
- Trim off any control pressure

- Maintain wings level with aileron, coordinate with rudder

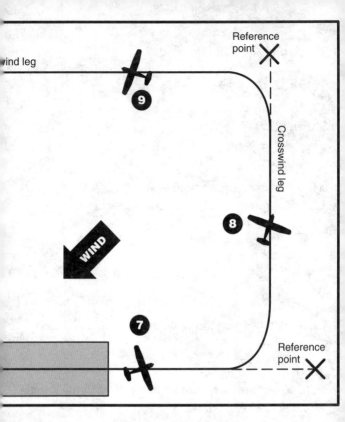

- Hold full aileron into wind

- Apply full throttle smoothly and positively

(continued)

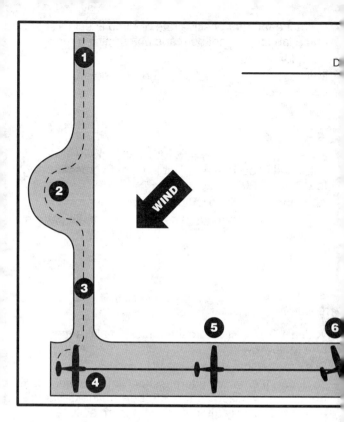

4

- Line up on runway centerline, nose wheel straight
- Check the windsock

- Select a reference point straight ahead for tracking
- Keep heels on floor, and toes on rudder pedals, not brakes

- Retract gear after positive rate of climb is established, and a landing cannot be made on remaining runway
- Scan for traffic
- Maintain a straight track over the extended runway centerline

- Beyond end of runway and within 300 feet of traffic pattern altitude, make a climbing turn to crosswind leg (bank angle 20° maximum)
- Allow for wind drift to keep a square pattern
- Maintain climb speed and continue to climb to pattern altitude
- Level off at pattern altitude
- Scan for traffic

- Within 1/2 to 1 mile from the runway, make a medium turn to downwind leg (bank angle 30° maximum)
- Scan for traffic
- To depart the traffic pattern, either climb straight out from the upwind leg, or turn 45° beyond the departure end of the runway after reaching pattern altitude

Evaluation:

- Use 0° (normal takeoff) flap setting
- Clear area and align airplane on runway centerline
- Advance throttle smoothly to takeoff power
- Rotate and lift off at the recommended airspeed and accelerate to V_Y
- Establish pitch attitude for V_Y and maintain V_Y during the climb (+10/-5 knots for Private and Sport, ±5 knots for Commercial and CFI)
- Retract landing gear after a positive rate of climb is established
- Maintain takeoff power to a safe maneuvering altitude
- Maintain directional control and proper wind-drift correction throughout takeoff and climb
- Comply with noise abatement procedures
- Complete the appropriate checklist

CROSSWIND TAKEOFF & CLIMB

(Private, Sport, Commercial, CFI)

Objective: Takeoff and climb out to the downwind leg of the traffic pattern with a crosswind component.

Task: Check Manufacturer Recommendations

- Complete preflight inspection (see Page 4)
- Verify crosswind component will not be exceeded
  *Manufacturer Recommended crosswind component
  _____ knots*
- Complete starting airplane check (see Page 6)
- Taxi to crosswind runway

- Complete before-takeoff check (see Page 6)
- Wing flaps 0° for crosswind takeoff

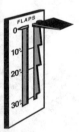

- Know local airport traffic pattern and altitude procedures

- Obtain takeoff and departure clearance, if required
- Look out and check that runway and approaches are all clear

5

- Keep straight with rudder
- Continue to hold aileron into wind and reduce deflection as speed increases
- Hold the nose wheel on the ground
- Check RPM for full power
- Check engine instruments are in the green arc

6

- Cleanly leave runway slightly above normal lift-off speed

  Manufacturer Recommended lift-off speed _____ knots

- Use right rudder to offset torque as required

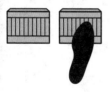

- Keep right hand on the throttle
- Turn into wind to correct for drift

7

- Establish attitude that results in V_Y with full throttle

  Manufacturer Recommended V_Y _____ knots

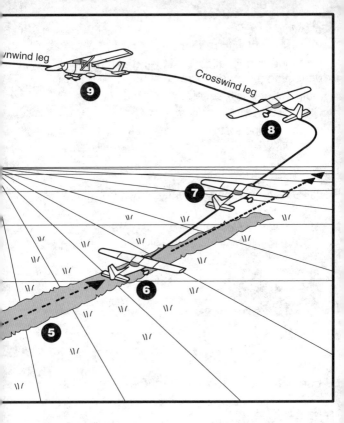

- During the takeoff ground run, keep weight off the nose wheel with control column held back

5

- Keep straight with rudder
- Keep wings level with aileron
- Check RPM for full power
- Check engine instruments are in the green arc
- Relax back pressure on control column as speed builds for earliest possible liftoff

(continued)

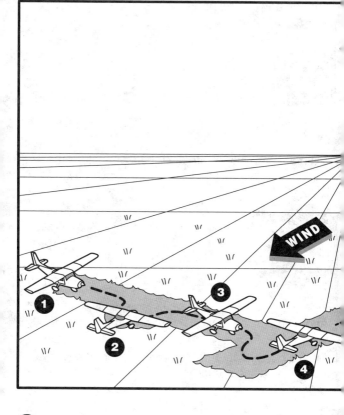

- Continue taxi roll without stopping and line up on runway centerline, nose wheel straight
- Select a reference point straight ahead for tracking
- Keep heels on floor, and toes on rudder pedals, not brakes

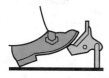

- Without stopping, apply full throttle smoothly and positively

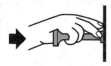

- Trim off any control pressure

- Maintain crab angle with aileron, coordinate with rudder

- Retract gear after positive rate of climb is established, and a landing cannot be made on remaining runway
- Scan for traffic
- Maintain a straight track over the extended runway centerline using a reference point

8

- Beyond end of runway and within 300 feet of traffic pattern altitude, make a climbing turn to crosswind leg (bank angle 20° maximum)
- Allow for wind drift by crabbing, to keep a square pattern
- Maintain climb speed and continue to climb to pattern altitude
- Level off at pattern altitude
- Scan for traffic

- Within 1/2 to 1 mile from runway, make a medium turn to downwind leg (bank angle 30° maximum)
- Continue to crab to correct for wind drift
- Scan for traffic
- To depart the traffic pattern, either climb straight out from the upwind leg, or turn 45° beyond the departure end of the runway after reaching pattern altitude

Evaluation:

- Use 0° (crosswind takeoff) flap setting
- Position the flight controls for existing wind conditions
- Clear area and align airplane on runway centerline
- Advance throttle smoothly to takeoff power
- Rotate and lift off at the recommended airspeed and accelerate to V_Y
- Establish pitch attitude for V_Y and maintain V_Y during the climb (+10/-5 knots for Private and Sport, ±5 knots for Commercial and CFI)
- Retract landing gear after a positive rate of climb is established
- Maintain takeoff power to a safe maneuvering altitude
- Maintain directional control and proper wind-drift correction throughout takeoff and climb
- Comply with noise abatement procedures
- Complete the appropriate checklist

SOFT-FIELD TAKEOFF & CLIMB

(Private, Sport, Commercial, CFI)

Objective: Get the airplane airborne as quickly as possible to eliminate drag caused by tall grass, sand, mud, and snow, and climb out to the downwind leg of the traffic pattern.

Task: Check Manufacturer Recommendations

- Complete preflight inspection (see Page 4)
- Complete starting airplane check (see Page 6)
- Taxi to upwind runway

- Complete before-takeoff check (see Page 6)
- Wing flaps 10° for soft-field takeoff

- Know local airport traffic pattern and altitude procedures

- Obtain takeoff and departure clearances, if required
- Look out and check that runway and approaches are all clear

- Once airborne, stay within 10 feet of the ground and accelerate in ground effect to V_Y
  Manufacturer Recommended V_Y _____ knots

- Climb out of ground effect at V_Y
- Use right rudder to offset torque as required

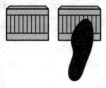

- Keep right hand on the throttle

- Trim off any control pressure

- Maintain wings level with aileron, coordinate with rudder

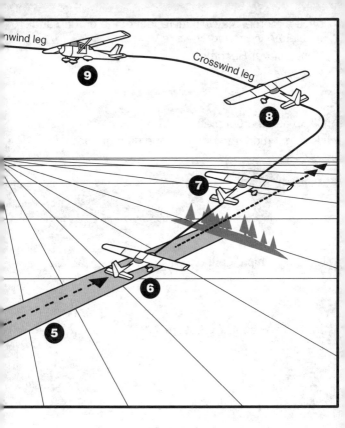

- Apply full throttle smoothly and positively

- Release brakes as full power is reached

5

- Keep straight with rudder
- Keep wings level with aileron
- Check RPM for full power
- Check engine instruments are in the green arc
- Keep airplane full weight on main wheels until lift-off speed is attained

(continued)

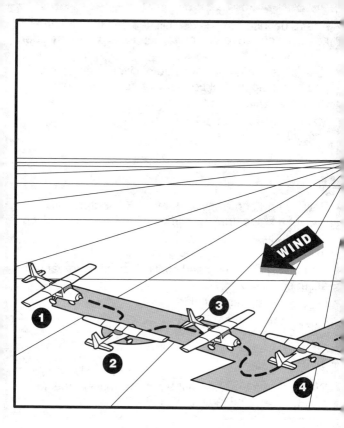

- Position airplane at the end of the runway to ensure maximum runway available, and align with runway centerline
- Select a reference point straight ahead for tracking
- Hold toes on the brakes

- After a definite climb is established and the airplane has accelerated to V_Y, retract flaps and adjust attitude to maintain V_Y
- Retract gear after positive rate of climb is established, and a landing cannot be made on remaining runway
- Scan for traffic
- Maintain a straight track over the extended runway centerline

8

- Beyond end of runway and within 300 feet of traffic pattern altitude, make a climbing turn to crosswind leg (bank angle 20° maximum)
- Allow for wind drift to keep a square pattern
- Maintain climb speed and continue to climb to pattern altitude
- Level off at pattern altitude
- Scan for traffic

9

- Within 1/2 to 1 mile from the runway, make a medium turn to downwind leg (bank angle 30° maximum)
- Scan for traffic
- To depart the traffic pattern, either climb straight out from the upwind leg, or turn 45° beyond the departure end of the runway after reaching pattern altitude

Evaluation:

- Position the flight controls for existing wind conditions and to maximize lift as quickly as possible
- Use 10° (soft-field takeoff) flap setting
- Clear the area
- Taxi onto the takeoff surface at a speed consistent with safety and align airplane on runway centerline without stopping while advancing the throttle smoothly to takeoff power
- Establish and maintain pitch attitude that will transfer the weight of the airplane from the wheels to the wings as rapidly as possible
- Lift off and remain in ground effect while accelerating to V_Y, be careful not to settle back to runway
- Establish pitch attitude for V_Y and maintain V_Y during the climb (+10/-5 knots for Private and Sport, ±5 knots for Commercial and CFI)
- Retract landing gear and flaps after a positive rate of climb is established
- Maintain takeoff power to a safe maneuvering altitude
- Maintain directional control and proper wind-drift correction throughout takeoff and climb
- Comply with noise abatement procedures
- Complete the appropriate checklist

SHORT-FIELD TAKEOFF & CLIMB

(Private, Sport, Commercial, CFI)

Objective: Takeoff in the shortest possible distance, clear obstacles at the end of the runway, ad climb out to the downwind leg of the traffic pattern.

Task: Check Manufacturer Recommendations

- Complete preflight inspection (see Page 4)
- Complete starting airplane check (see Page 6)
- Taxi to upwind runway

2

- Complete before-takeoff check (see Page 6)
- Wing flaps 10° for short-field takeoff, or as recommended

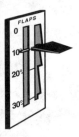

- Know local airport traffic pattern and altitude procedures

- Obtain takeoff and departure clearances, if required
- Look out and check that runway and approaches are all clear

- Lift off at minimum recommended flying speed
  *Manufacturer Recommended minimum lift-offspeed
  _____ knots*

- Use right rudder to offset torque as required
- Keep right hand on throttle

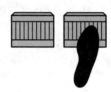

- Establish the attitude that results in V_X with full throttle
  Manufacturer Recommended V_X _____ knots
- Maintain wings level with aileron, coordinate with rudder

- Retract flaps at a safe altitude and when clear of obstacles
- Retract gear after positive rate of climb is established, and a landing cannot be made on remaining runway
- Increase climb speed to V_Y
  Manufacturer Recommended V_Y _____ knots

- Set movable dot on the attitude indicator to horizon line and maintain constant attitude

- Check altimeter for constant altitude. Make small corrections with elevator (yoke). Make larger corrections immediately with coordinated pitch and throttle.

- Vertical speed indicator should remain at 0

- For VFR flights, use outside visual cues as primary reference, cockpit instruments as secondary reference and as a cross-check (look outside, peek inside)
- Check fuel and engine gauges periodically

Evaluation:
- Maintain a definite heading, ±10°
- Maintain a definite altitude, ±100 feet
- Use definite power setting and airspeed, ±10 knots
- Trim for level flight
- For altitude deviations of less than 100 feet, correct with pitch; if you are off by more than 100 feet, use pitch and a small throttle adjustment
- In turbulence, use maneuvering speed (V_A)
- Use left hand on yoke, controlling yoke with thumb and two fingers and making tiny corrections
- Make smooth and coordinated control applications

- If left wing is low, correct by using light right aileron plus right rudder pressure

- If right wing is low, correct by using light left aileron plus left rudder pressure

 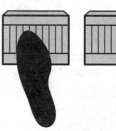

- After corrections, neutralize controls and trim airplane
- Check airspeed indicator for constant airspeed

- Check heading indicator for constant heading

- Maintain coordination by keeping the ball in center

- Trim off any control pressure

- Scan for traffic
- Maintain a straight track over the extended runway centerline

8

- Beyond end of runway and within 300 feet of traffic pattern altitude, make a climbing turn to crosswind leg (bank angle 20° maximum)
- Allow for wind drift to keep a square pattern
- Maintain climb speed and continue to climb to pattern altitude
- Level off at pattern altitude
- Scan for traffic

9

- Within 1/2 to 1 mile from runway, make a medium turn to downwind leg (bank angle 30° maximum)
- Scan for traffic
- To depart the traffic pattern, either climb straight out from the upwind leg, or turn 45° beyond the departure end of the runway after reaching pattern altitude

Evaluation:

- Position flight controls for existing wind conditions
- Use 10° (short-field takeoff) flap setting
- Clear the area
- Taxi into the takeoff position to allow maximum utilization of available takeoff area and align the airplane on runway centerline
- Advance throttle smoothly to takeoff power
- Rotate at recommended airspeed, lift off, and accelerate to the recommended obstacle clearance airspeed or V_X
- Establish pitch attitude for the recommended obstacle clearance airspeed or V_X and maintain that airspeed, (+10/-5 knots for Private and Sport, +5/-0 knots for Commercial and CFI) until the obstacle is cleared, or until airplane is 50 feet above the surface
- After clearing the obstacle, accelerate to V_Y, establish pitch attitude for V_Y, and maintain V_Y during the climb (+10/-5 knots for Private and Sport, ±5 for Commercial and CFI)
- Retract landing gear and flaps after a positive rate of climb is established
- Maintain takeoff power to a safe maneuvering altitude
- Maintain directional control and proper wind-drift correction throughout takeoff and climb
- Comply with noise abatement procedures
- Complete the appropriate checklist

STRAIGHT & LEVEL FLIGHT

(Private, Sport, Commercial, CFI)

Objective: Maintain a constant heading and altitude.

Task:
- Adjust power to cruise RPM

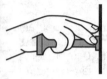

- Trim airplane to maintain hands-off attitude

- Select an outside reference
- Maintain airplane nose constant in relation to the horizon, and wing tips equidistant above horizon

SHALLOW & MEDIUM TURNS

(Private, Sport, Commercial, CFI)

Objective: Change or return to a desired heading by entering, maintaining, and rolling out of a shallow (0–20°) or medium (20–45°) level turn, using constant power and holding a constant altitude.

Task:

- Go to practice area where terrain is appropriate for maneuvering, and emergency landing area is available
- Set power to obtain maneuvering speed (V_A)
  Manufacturer Recommended V_A _____ knots
- Select an altitude to maintain
- Clear area for other aircraft
- Trim airplane for level hands-off flight
- Select a heading or reference point for rollout

2

- Look outside, peek inside
- From straight-and-level flight, coordinate aileron and rudder to roll in direction of turn

- Due to torque effect, more rudder is required for right turns
- Exert slight back pressure on the control column to maintain altitude

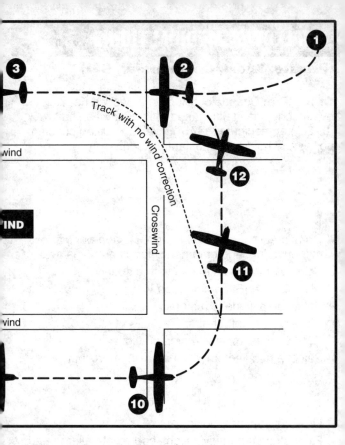

Track with no wind correction

Crosswind

wind

IND

wind

- Maintain coordination and crab into the wind

- Same airspeed, medium ground speed
- Maintain distance from boundary

(continued)

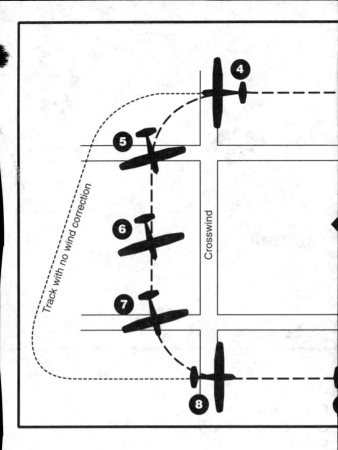

Track with no wind correction

Crosswind

3

- Same indicated airspeed, fastest ground speed
- Maintain distance from boundary
- Crab angle is not required

4

- Steepest turn for fastest ground speed (maximum bank angle 45°)
- Ease off bank angle as the wind turns to a crosswind, and ground speed begins to slow

5

- Roll out of the turn wings-level, crabbing into the wind
- Turn will be more than 90°

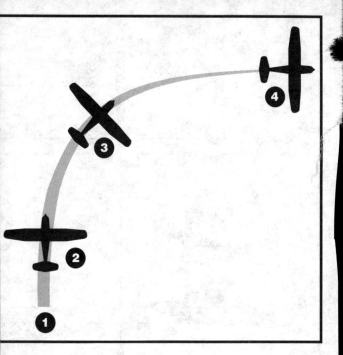

3

Look outside, peek inside
Select a spot on the horizon to maintain altitude and
bank angle

Maintain bank angle with aileron
(reference attitude indicator)

Maintain coordination with rudder
(reference turn coordinator)

- Maintain altitude with the elevator, using back pressure on the control column (reference altimeter)

4

- Look outside, peek inside

- Anticipate rollout heading or reference point

- Roll out of the bank with aileron and coordinated rudder pressure, to return to straight-and-level flight

- Release elevator back pressure

Evaluation:
- Left turns are performed in the same manner as right turns
- Practice both right and left turns, returning to straight-and-level flight
- Roll out to predetermined headings
- Maintain altitude, ±100 feet
- Maintain bank angle, ±5°
- Maintain rollout heading, ±10°
- Maintain coordination at all times

RECTANGULAR COURSE

(Private, Sport, CFI)

Objective: Fly a ground track equidistant from all sides of a selected rectangular area on the ground, accounting for wind effects, and maintaining a constant altitude and airspeed.

Task:

- Find practice area where terrain is appropriate for maneuvering, emergency landing area available
- Select a rectangular area, 1/2 to 1 mile in length
- Set power to obtain maneuvering speed (V_A)
  Manufacturer Recommended V_A _____ knots

- Maintain traffic pattern altitude, 600 to 1,000 feet AGL
- Clear area for other aircraft

DO NOT FORGET CLEARING TURNS

- Trim airplane for level hands-off flight

- Enter the maneuver 45° to downwind, with first circuit to the left

7

- Start the turn with a medium bank angle
  Reduce bank angle as ground speed slows

8

- Roll out wings-level, directly upwind
- Turn will be less than 90° to upwind leg

9

- Same indicated airspeed, slowest ground speed
- Maintain distance from boundary
- Crab angle is not required

10

- Start a shallow turn for the slowest ground speed
- Gradually increase to a medium bank angle as the ground speed increases
- Roll out wings-level with a wind correction angle and crab into the wind

11

- Turn will be less than 90°
- Same indicated airspeed, medium ground speed
- Maintain coordination and crab into the wind

12

- Start a medium turn, gradually increasing bank angle as ground speed increases
- Turn will be more than 90°
- Exit at point of entry at the same altitude and airspeed at which the maneuver was started, and reverse course

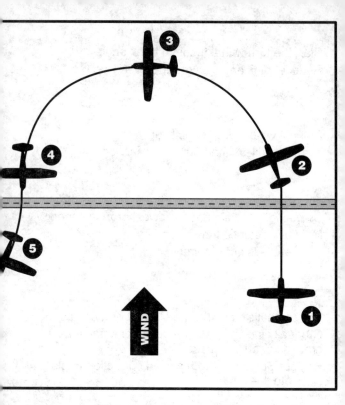

Evaluation:

- Determine wind direction and speed
- Select reference line with an emergency landing area within gliding distance
- Plan maneuver to enter at 600 to 1,000 feet AGL, perpendicular to the selected reference line, downwind, with the first series of turns to the left
- Apply adequate wind-drift correction to track a constant-radius half-circle on each side of the selected reference line
- Divide attention between airplane control and ground track; maintain coordinated flight
- Reverse course, as directed, and exit at point of entry at the same altitude and airspeed at which the maneuver was started
- Maintain altitude (±100 feet for Private and Sport), maintain airspeed (±10 knots for Private and Sport)

S-TURNS

(Private, Sport, CFI)

Objective: Fly a series of S-turns across a line ground feature, with semicircles of equal size, accounting for wind effects, and maintaining a constant altitude and airspeed.

Task:

- Find practice area where terrain is appropriate for maneuvering, emergency landing area available
- Select a line feature that lies crosswind
- Set power to obtain maneuvering speed (V_A)
  Manufacturer Recommended V_A _____ knots
- Maintain and fly an altitude between 600 and 1,000 feet AGL
- Clear area for other aircraft
- Trim airplane for level hands-off flight
- Approach the line feature downwind

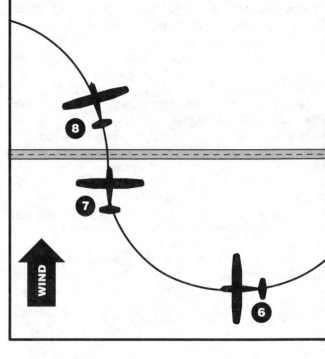

DO NOT FORGET CLEARING TURNS

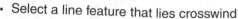

- Cross the line feature wings-level
- Initial turn is to the left
- Highest ground speed
- Steepest bank angle (do not exceed 45°)

- Moderate bank angle and decreasing as airplane begins to turn upwind
- Maintain coordination throughout maneuver

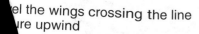

- el the wings crossing the line
- ure upwind

s

- Slowest ground speed
- Turn in opposite direction
- Shallowest bank angle

- Moderate bank angle and increasing as airplane begins to turn downwind

- Level the wings crossing the line feature downwind

- Fastest ground speed
- Exit maneuver at the same altitude and airspeed at which the maneuver was started

valuation:

The closer the track of the airplane is to the field boundaries, the steeper the bank at the turning points

Determine wind direction and speed

Select ground reference area with an emergency landing area within gliding distance

Plan maneuver to enter at traffic pattern altitude, 600 to 1,000 feet AGL, at an appropriate distance from the selected reference area, 45° to the downwind leg, with the first circuit to the left

Apply adequate wind-drift correction during straight and turning flight to maintain a constant ground track around the rectangular reference area

Divide attention between airplane control and ground track, maintain coordinated flight

Exit at point of entry at the same altitude and airspeed at which the maneuver was started, and reverse course

Maintain altitude (±100 feet for Private and Sport), maintain airspeed (±10 knots for Private and Sport)

TURNS AROUND A POINT

(Private, Sport, CFI)

Objective: Fly two or more complete circles of uniform radii or distance from a ground reference point by varying the bank angle to account for wind effects, while maintaining a constant altitude and airspeed.

Task:

1

- Find practice area where terrain is appropriate for maneuvering, emergency landing area available
- Select a reference point
- Set power to obtain maneuvering speed (V_A)
  Manufacturer Recommended V_A _____ knots
- Maintain an altitude between 600 and 1,000 feet AGL
- Clear area for other aircraft

DO NOT FORGET CLEARING TURNS

- Trim airplane for level hands-off flight

- Approach reference point downwind

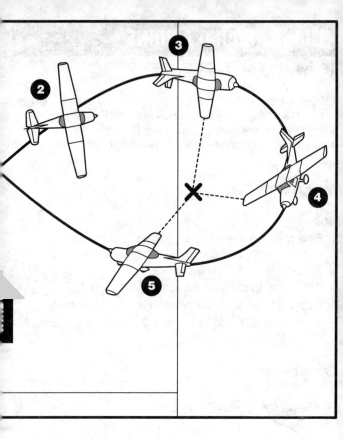

- Prevent apparent fore-aft movement of the pylon using elevator

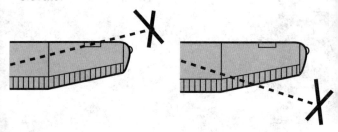

- Follow pylon with the control column

(continued)

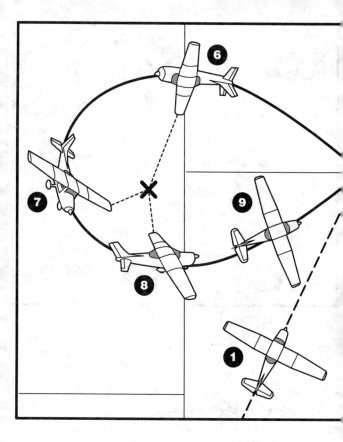

- Just past the right pylon, roll into a right turn (30-40° at the steepest point) to position the wing tip on the pylon

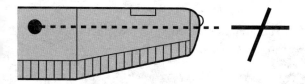

- Prevent apparent up-down movement of the pylon using aileron

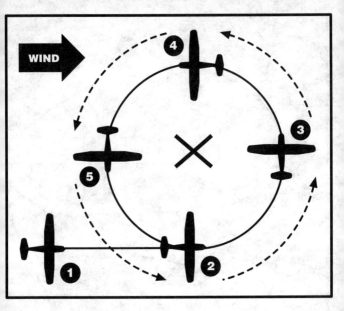

2

- Initial turn is to the left
- Highest ground speed
- Steepest bank angle (do not exceed 45°)
- Maintain distance from reference point

3

- Gradually decrease bank angle as airplane begins to turn upwind
- Maintain distance from reference point
- Maintain coordination throughout maneuver

4

- Slowest ground speed
- Shallowest bank angle
- Maintain distance from reference point

5

- Gradually increase bank angle as airplane begins to turn downwind
- Maintain distance from reference point
- Fly at least two turns, and exit at point of entry at the same altitude and airspeed at which the maneuver was started
- Reverse course as directed

Evaluation:

- Determine wind direction and speed
- Select reference point with an emergency landing area within gliding distance
- Plan maneuver to enter at 600 to 1,000 feet AGL, at an appropriate distance from the reference point, with the airplane headed downwind and the first turn to the left
- Apply adequate wind-drift correction to track a constant-radius turn around the selected reference point
- Divide attention between airplane control and ground track; maintain coordinated flight
- Complete two turns, exit at point of entry at the same altitude and airspeed at which the maneuver was started, and reverse course as directed
- Maintain altitude (±100 feet for Private and Sport), maintain airspeed (±10 knots for Private and Sport)

EIGHTS-ON-PYLONS

(Commercial, CFI)

Objective: Fly a figure-8 pattern while maintaining the wing tip in line with the reference point by varying altitude, bank angle, and airspeed.

Task:

- Find practice area where terrain is appropriate for maneuvering, emergency landing area available
- Select 2 pylons approximately 1/2-mile apart, perpendicular to the wind
- Set power to obtain maneuvering speed (V_A)
  Manufacturer Recommended V_A _____ *knots*
- Obtain the wind speed and direction
- Calculate the pivotal altitude for entry downwind (highest ground speed)
  Pivotal altitude = (ground speed in knots)^2/11.3

Ground speed	Pivotal altitude AGL
120 knots	_____
110 knots	_____
100 knots	_____
90 knots	_____
80 knots	_____

- Clear area for other aircraft

DO NOT FORGET CLEARING TURNS

- Trim airplane for level hands-off fight
- Enter maneuver by approaching the midpoint of the pylons diagonally, with the wind from the side and behind (so ground speed will be high)

3

- Crosswind, ground speed decreases
- If pylon moves forward of your line-of-sight along the wing tip, apply forward pressure to descend

  Maintain coordination; do not use rudder pressure to "hold" pylon

4

- Upwind, slowest ground speed
- Shallowest bank
- Lowest pivotal altitude

5

- Downwind, fastest ground speed
- Steepest bank (30–40° at steepest point)
- Highest pivotal altitude
- Cross midpoint of pylons wings-level

6

- Just past the left pylon, roll into a left turn to position wing tip on the pylon
- Prevent up-down movement of the pylon using aileron
- Prevent fore-aft movement of the pylon using elevator
- Follow pylon with the control column

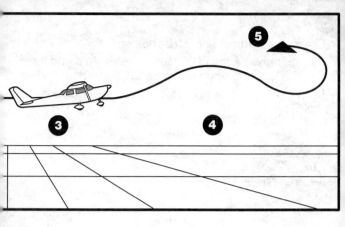

Evaluation:

- Select an entry altitude that will allow the task to be completed no lower than 1,500 feet AGL or the recommended altitude, whichever is higher
- Maintain airspeed at which the airplane is capable of maintaining controlled flight without activating a stall warning, approximately 5–10 knots above 1G stall speed
- Accomplish coordinated straight-and-level flight and level turns, at bank angles and in configurations as specified
- Divide attention between airplane control and orientation
- Maintain specified altitude (±100 feet for Private and Sport, ±50 feet for Commercial); specified heading (±10° for Private, Sport, and Commercial), specified airspeed (+10/-0 knots for Private and Sport, +5/-0 knots for Commercial), and specified angle of bank (±10° for Private and Sport, ±5° for Commercial)

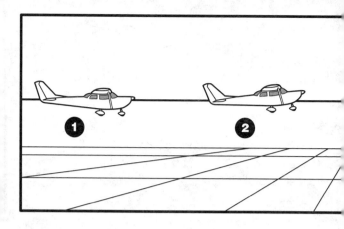

- Maintain directional control, using outside visual references
- Practice gentle climb, descents and turns at a constant airspeed
- Practice lowering flaps (in small increments) and gear
- Controls are less effective at slower speeds

- Raise flaps (in small increments) and gear
- Increase power to achieve cruise speed

- Reduce angle of attack by lowering the nose to maintain altitude

- Carburetor heat off (fully in)

- Maintain coordination (reduce pressure on right rudder)

- Trim airplane for normal cruise condition

7

- Upwind, slowest ground speed
- Shallowest bank
- Lowest pivotal altitude

8

- Downwind, fastest ground speed
- Steepest bank (30–40° at the steepest point)
- Highest pivotal altitude

9

- Cross midpoint of pylons wings-level
- Repeat the figure-8 pattern
- Exit at point of entry at the same altitude and airspeed at which the maneuver was started

Evaluation:

- Determine the approximate pivotal altitude
- Select suitable pylons that will permit straight-and-level flight between the pylons, considering emergency landing areas
- Attain proper configuration and airspeed prior to entry; enter the maneuver at the appropriate altitude and airspeed and at a bank angle not to exceed 40° at the steepest point.
- Apply necessary corrections so that the line-of-sight reference line remains on the pylon with minimum longitudinal movement
- Exhibit proper orientation, division of attention, and planning
- Apply the necessary wind-effect correction to track properly between pylons
- Hold pylons using appropriate pivotal altitude, avoiding slips and skids

MANEUVERING DURING SLOW FLIGHT

(Private, Sport, Commercial, CFI)

Objective: Establish slow flight, and then maneuver the airplane at airspeeds just above stall speed, without stalling.

Task: Check Manufacturer Recommendations

- Find practice area where terrain is appropriate for maneuvering, emergency landing area available
- Select an altitude that allows maneuver to be performed no lower than 1,500 feet AGL
- Clear area for other aircraft
- Trim airplane for level hands-off flight

DO NOT FORGET CLEARING TURNS

2

- Carburetor heat on (fully out), or as required
- Reduce power
- Apply back pressure on yoke to reduce airspeed and maintain altitude
- Maintain coordination with rudder pressure (more right rudder needed to counteract torque)

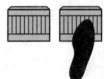

- As airspeed approaches stall speed, add power
- Use power to maintain altitude
- Use pitch attitude to control airspeed, approximately 5–10 knots above 1G stall speed
- Maintain coordination with rudder pressure
- Trim airplane for slow flight condition

POWER-OFF STALLS

(Private, Sport, Commercial, CFI)

Objective: Stall the airplane, without power, in the landing configuration, then recover with a minimum loss of altitude.

Task: Check Manufacturer Recommendations

- Find practice area where terrain is appropriate for maneuvering, emergency landing area available
- Select an altitude that allows maneuver to be completed no lower than 1,500 feet AGL
- Clear area for other aircraft
- Trim airplane for level hands-off flight

DO NOT FORGET CLEARING TURNS

❷

- Carburetor heat on (fully out), or as required

- Power to IDLE (throttle fully out)

- Apply back pressure on yoke to reduce airspeed and maintain altitude

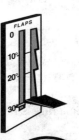

- Set flaps for landing configuration (make sure airspeed is within white arc on airspeed indicator)

- Maintain coordination with rudder pressure (more right rudder needed to counteract torque)

- Maintain ailerons neutral
- Continue to bring the yoke back

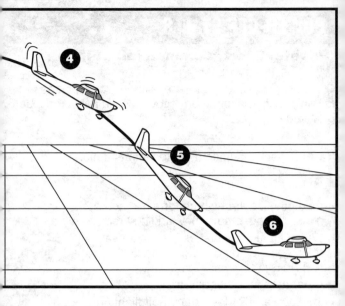

- Maintain wings-level and coordination
- Recognize and announce symptoms of approaching stall
- Airspeed and noise level decrease
- Flight controls are less effective, feel "mushy"
- Stall warning system activated (light, horn, or buzzer)
- Airframe begins to buffet
- Attitude is nose high

- Maintain wings-level and coordination
- Recognize and announce the full stall
- Yoke is fully back
- Sink rate is high, and airplane pitches down

(continued)

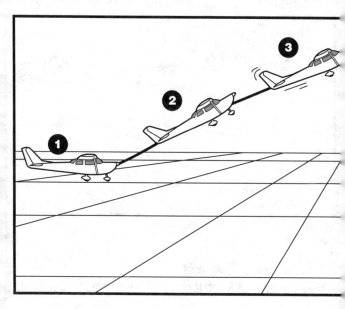

- Maintain ailerons neutral
- Continue to bring the yoke back (nose will be higher than in a power-off stall)

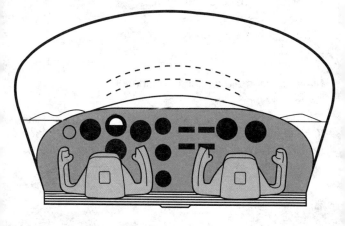

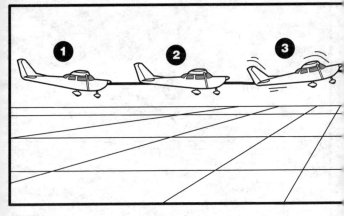

3
- Maintain wings-level and coordination
- Recognize and announce symptoms of approaching stall
- Airspeed and noise level decrease
- Flight controls are less effective, feel "mushy"
- Stall warning system activated (light, horn, or buzzer)
- Airframe begins to buffet
- Attitude is nose high

4
- Maintain wings-level and coordination
- Recognize and announce full stall
- Yoke is fully back
- Sink rate is high, and airplane pitches down

5
- Release the back pressure on the yoke
- Add full power (throttle fully in)

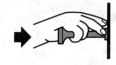

- Carburetor heat off (fully in)

- Level the wings with coordinated aileron and rudder

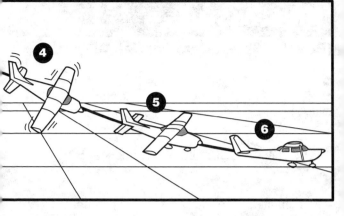

- Retract flaps (in increments) as airspeed reaches V_Y
- Resume normal flight attitude, power, and airspeed with minimum loss of altitude
- Practice stall in straight flight and while in a turn

Evaluation:

- Select an entry altitude that allows task to be completed no lower than 1,500 feet AGL or the recommended altitude, whichever is higher
- Establish a stabilized approach in the approach or landing configuration, as specified
- Transition smoothly from approach or landing attitude to pitch attitude that will induce a stall
- Maintain a specified heading, ±10° in straight flight; maintain a specified angle of bank, not to exceed 20°, (±10° for Private and Sport, ±5° for Commercial), in turning flight while inducing the stall
- Recognize and recover promptly after a fully developed stall occurs
- Recover promptly after stall occurs by simultaneously decreasing pitch attitude, applying power, and leveling wings to return to a straight-and-level flight attitude with a minimum loss of altitude appropriate for airplane
- Retract flaps to the recommended setting; retract landing gear, if retractable, after a positive rate of climb is established; accelerate to V_Y before the final flap retraction; return to the altitude, heading, and airspeed as specified

POWER-ON STALLS

(Private, Sport, Commercial, CFI)

Objective: Stall the airplane with power, in the takeoff configuration, then recover with a minimum loss of altitude.

Task: Check Manufacturer Recommendations

- Find practice area where terrain is appropriate for maneuvering, emergency landing area available
- Select an altitude that allows maneuver to be completed no lower than 1,500 feet AGL
- Clear area for other aircraft
- Trim airplane for level hands-off flight

DO NOT FORGET CLEARING TURNS

2

- Slow airplane to lift-off speed
  Manufacturer Recommended lift-off speed _____ knots
- Apply back pressure on yoke to establish takeoff configuration

- Apply takeoff power
- Maintain coordination with rudder pressure (more right rudder needed to counteract torque)

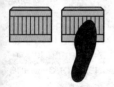

- Release back pressure on the yoke

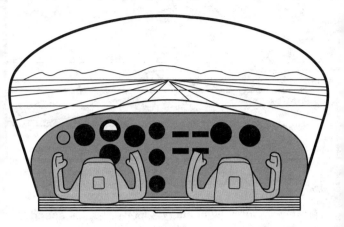

- Level the wings with coordinated aileron and rudder

6

- Resume normal flight attitude, power, and airspeed with minimum loss of altitude
- Practice stall in straight flight and while in a turn

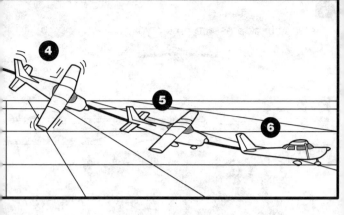

- Resume normal flight attitude, power, and airspeed with minimum loss of altitude
- Practice stall in straight flight, in a turn, power-on, and power-off

Evaluation:

- Select an entry altitude that allows task to be completed no lower than 3,000 feet AGL
- Establish the airplane in a steady flight condition, airspeed below V_A, 20 knots above unaccelerated stall speed or the manufacturer's recommendations
- Transition smoothly from the cruise attitude to the angle of bank of approximately 45° that will induce a stall
- Maintain coordinated turning flight, increasing elevator back pressure steadily and firmly to induce the stall
- Recognize and recover promptly at the onset of a stall by simultaneously reducing the angle of bank, decreasing pitch, increasing power as appropriate, and leveling the wings to return to a straight-and-level flight attitude with a minimum loss of altitude appropriate for the airplane
- Return to the altitude, heading, and airspeed specified

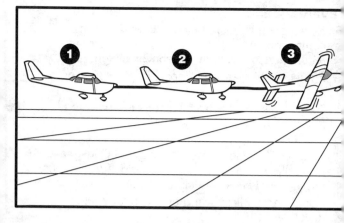

 3

- Smoothly and steadily increase back-elevator pressure
- After the airspeed reaches the design maneuvering speed or within 20 knots above the unaccelerated stall speed, increase back elevator pressure firmly until a definite stall occurs

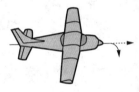

 4

- Centrifugal force will push the pilot's body down in the seat, increase the wing loading, and decrease the airspeed
- Observe speed restrictions to prevent exceeding the load limit of the airplane

 5

- Release the back pressure on the yoke
- Add full power (throttle fully in)

- Carburetor heat off (fully in)

- Level the wings with coordinated aileron and rudder

Evaluation:

- Select an entry altitude that allows task to be completed no lower than 1,500 feet AGL or the recommended altitude, whichever is higher
- Establish the takeoff or departure configuration, airspeed, and power as specified
- Transition smoothly from takeoff or departure attitude to the pitch attitude that will induce a stall
- Maintain a specified heading (±10° for Private and Sport, ±5° for Commercial) in straight flight; maintain a specified angle of bank, not to exceed 20°, ±10°, in turning flight while inducing the stall
- Recognize and recover promptly after a fully developed stall occurs
- Recover promptly after a stall occurs by simultaneously decreasing the pitch attitude, applying power as appropriate, and leveling the wings to return to a straight-and-level flight attitude with a minimum loss of altitude appropriate for the airplane
- Retract flaps to the recommended setting; retract landing gear, if retractable, after a positive rate of climb is established; accelerate to V_Y before the final flap retraction; return to the altitude, heading, and airspeed as specified

ACCELERATED STALLS

(Commercial and CFI)

Objective: Demonstrate how stalls result from attempts to fly at excessively high angles of attack, recognize, and recover promptly.

Task: Check Manufacturer Recommendations

- Find practice area where terrain is appropriate for maneuvering, emergency landing area available
- Select an altitude that allows maneuver to be completed no lower than 3,000 feet AGL
- Clear area for other aircraft
- Trim airplane for level hands-off flight

DO NOT FORGET CLEARING TURNS

- Carburetor heat on (fully out), or as required

- Establish the airplane in a steady flight condition, airspeed below V_A, 20 knots above unaccelerated stall speed or the manufacturer's recommendations

- Transition smoothly from the cruise attitude to the angle of bank of approximately 45° that will induce a stall

CROSSED-CONTROL STALLS

(CFI only)

Objective: Demonstrate the effect of improper control technique and emphasize the importance of using coordinated control pressures whenever making turns.

Task: Check Manufacturer Recommendations

- Find practice area where terrain is appropriate for maneuvering, emergency landing area available
- Select an altitude that allows maneuver to be completed no lower than 1,500 feet AGL—have plenty of altitude available for recovery
- Clear area for other aircraft
- Lower landing gear, if retractable
- DO NOT extend flaps
- Trim airplane for level hands-off flight

DO NOT FORGET CLEARING TURNS

- Carburetor heat on (fully out), or as required

- Power to IDLE (throttle fully out)

- Establish glide speed and attitude
  Manufacturer Recommended best glide speed _____ knots
- Re-trim airplane for gliding attitude
- Roll into medium-banked turn to simulate an overshot turn to final approach

- Apply excessive rudder in the direction of turn
- Maintain a constant bank by applying opposite aileron pressure

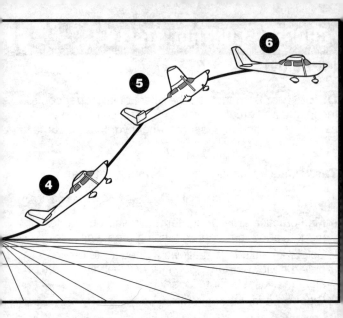

- With airplane held in the normal climbing attitude, adjust trim to relieve the heavy control pressures

- Maintain wings-level with coordinated aileron and rudder

6

- Complete normal go-around and level-off procedures
- Retract gear and flaps (in increments) as airspeed reaches V_Y
- Resume normal flight attitude, power, and airspeed with minimum loss of altitude

Evaluation:

- Demonstrate and simultaneously explain elevator trim stalls, in selected landing gear and flap configurations, from an instructional standpoint
- Analyze and correct simulated common errors related to elevator trim stalls in selected landing gear and flap configurations

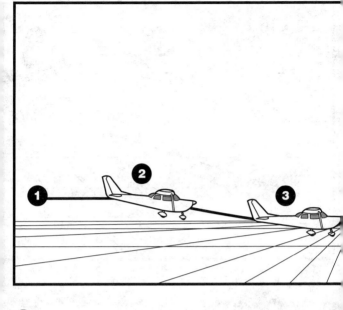

- Advance throttle smoothly to maximum power

- Carburetor heat off (fully in)

- The combined force of thrust, torque, and back elevator trim cause the nose to rise sharply and turn to the left
- Do not attempt to correct these forces

- When pitch attitude increases above the normal climbing attitude, and it is apparent a stall is imminent, apply forward pressure to the control column

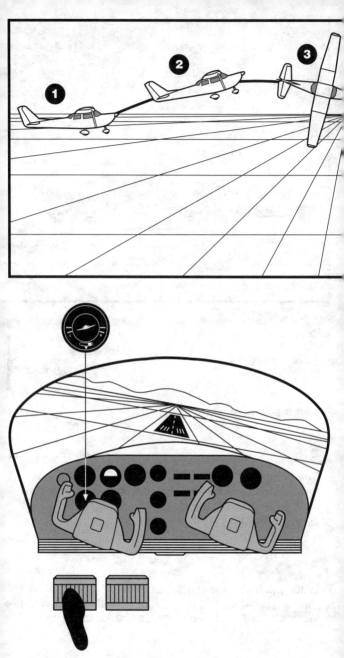

- Increase back elevator pressure to keep nose from lowering

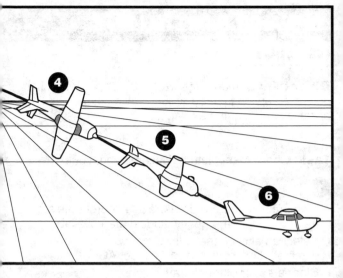

- Continue to increase control pressures until airplane stalls
- The stall might break toward or away from the turn, or snap into a spin
- Initiate recovery at the full stall

- Release the control pressures
- Add full power (throttle fully in)
- Carburetor heat off (fully in)

- Level the wings with coordinated aileron and rudder
- Resume normal flight attitude, power, and airspeed with minimum loss of altitude

Evaluation:

- Demonstrate and simultaneously explain a crossed-control stall, with landing gear extended, from an instructional standpoint
- Analyze and correct simulated common errors related to a crossed-control stall with landing gear extended

ELEVATOR TRIM STALLS

(CFI only)

Objective: Demonstrate what can happen when full power is applied for a go-around while not maintaining positive control of the airplane.

Task: Check Manufacturer Recommendations

- Find practice area where terrain is appropriate for maneuvering, emergency landing area available
- Select an altitude that allows maneuver to be completed no lower than 1,500 feet AGL
- Clear area for other aircraft
- Extend landing gear
- Extend flaps, 1/2 to full
- Trim airplane for level hands-off flight

DO NOT FORGET CLEARING TURNS

- Carburetor heat on (fully out), or as required

- Power to IDLE (throttle fully out)

- Establish glide attitude and best glide speed
  Manufacturer Recommended best glide speed _____ knots

- Re-trim airplane for the glide, as would be done during a landing approach (nose-up trim)

SECONDARY STALLS

(CFI only)

Objective: Demonstrate what happens when stall recovery is attempted before the airplane has regained sufficient flying speed.

Task: Check Manufacturer Recommendations

- Find practice area where terrain is appropriate for maneuvering, emergency landing area available
- Select an altitude that allows maneuver to be completed no lower than 1,500 feet AGL
- Clear area for other aircraft

DO NOT FORGET CLEARING TURNS

- Perform a stall

- At full stall, release back pressure

- Pull back on the control column before the airplane has regained sufficient flying speed

(continued)

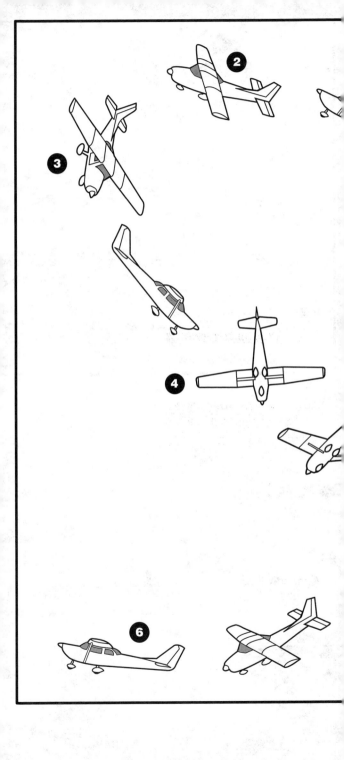

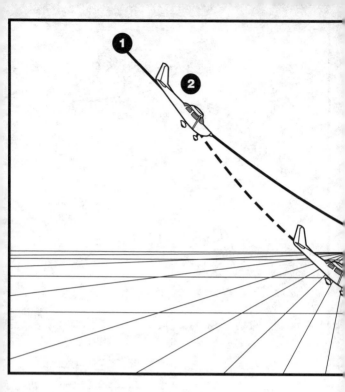

- Allow airplane to stall for a second time
- At full stall, release back pressure
- Add full power

4

- Maintain wings-level with coordinated aileron and rudder

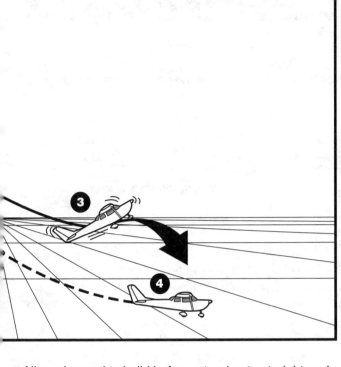

- Allow airspeed to build before returning to straight-and-level flight
- Resume normal flight attitude, power, and airspeed with minimum loss of altitude
- Practice from both a power-on and power-off stalled condition

Evaluation:

- Demonstrate and simultaneously explain secondary stalls, in selected landing gear and flap configuration, from an instructional standpoint
- Analyze and correct simulated common errors related to secondary stalls in selected landing gear and flap configurations

SPINS

(CFI only)

Objective: Enter, maintain, and recover from a spin, in order to prevent them, and know the proper procedure for recovering from unintentional spins.

Task: Check Manufacturer Recommendations

- Find practice area where terrain is appropriate for maneuvering, emergency landing area available
- Select an altitude that allows maneuver to be completed no lower than 1,500 feet AGL
- Clear area for other aircraft
- Trim airplane for level hands-off flight
- Carburetor heat on (fully out) as required

DO NOT FORGET CLEARING TURNS

- Power to IDLE (throttle fully out)

- Apply back pressure on yoke to reduce airspeed and maintain altitude

2

- Maintain ailerons neutral
- Just prior to stall, apply full rudder in the direction of the intended spin
- Continue to bring yoke fully back

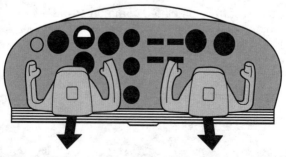

3

- Maintain full back pressure on the control column
- Maintain full rudder in the direction of spin

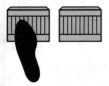

- Hold ailerons neutral
- Use outside references to maintain orientation throughout spin

4

- Keep throttle at IDLE (fully out)
- Maintain neutral ailerons
- Check spin direction (with outside reference and turn coordinator)
- Begin spin recovery 1/4 to 1/2 turn prior to desired recovery heading

5

- Verify power is IDLE
- Apply full rudder opposite the direction of the rotation

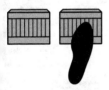

- Release back pressure, and then apply forward pressure on yoke to break the stall

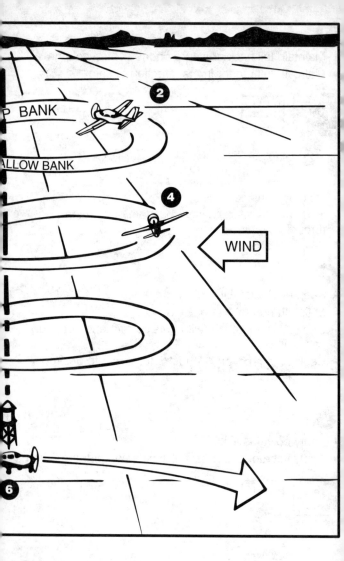

BANK

ALLOW BANK

2

4

WIND

6

4

- Highest ground speed
- Steepest bank angle (do not exceed 60°)
- Lowest pitch attitude to maintain constant airspeed
- Note wind conditions as altitude changes
- Maintain uniform radius around reference point

(continued)

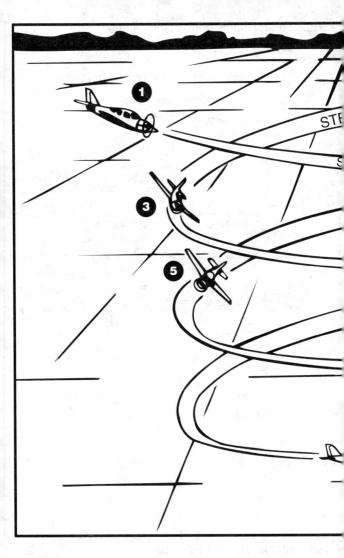

- Gradually decrease bank angle as airplane begins to turn upwind
- Maintain distance from reference point
- Briefly advance throttle to normal cruise power to clear engine
- Maintain constant airspeed
- Maintain coordination throughout maneuver

- Hold control inputs until rotation stops
- Neutralize rudder and level the wings when rotation stops
- Apply back pressure on the control column to recover from the ensuing dive

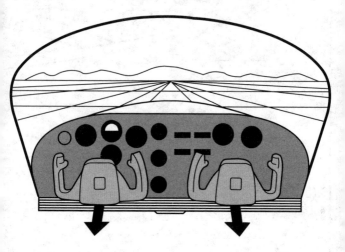

6

- Avoid a secondary stall or spin during the recovery
- As the nose rises past the horizon, add power

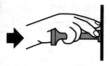

- Carburetor heat off
- Resume normal flight attitude, power, and airspeed with minimum loss of altitude

Evaluation:

- Demonstrate and simultaneously explain a spin (one turn) from an instructional standpoint
- Analyze and correct simulated common errors related to spins

Spin Awareness
(Private, Sport and Commercial)

- Exhibit knowledge of elements related to spin awareness by explaining—
    a. flight situations where unintentional spins may occur
    b. technique used to recognize and recover from unintentional spins
    c. recommended spin recovery procedure for the airplane used for the practical test
    d. aerodynamic factors, including instrument indications, that occur in a spin
    e. phases of a spin with regard to uncoordinated flight, the vertical and rotational velocities, and its rotation about the axis perpendicular to the earth's surface

STEEP SPIRALS

(Commercial, CFI)

Objective: Demonstrate a constant gliding turn, executing a series of three 360° turns while maintaining a ground reference point by varying the bank angle to account for wind effects, and maintaining a constant airspeed.

Task: Check Manufacturer Recommendations

- Find terrain where terrain is appropriate for maneuvering, emergency landing area available
- Select an altitude that allows spiral to be continued through a series of at least three 360° turns, to be performed no lower than 1,000 feet AGL
- Clear area for other aircraft
- Select a heading or reference point for rollout
- Close throttle
- Establish glide speed
  Manufacturer Recommended best glide speed _____ knots
- From straight-and-level flight into the wind, coordinate aileron and rudder to roll into a shallow turn around the selected spot on the ground

- Gradually increase bank angle as airplane begins to turn downwind
- Maintain distance from reference point
- Adjust attitude to maintain best glide speed
- Adjust bank angle to maintain a uniform radius

- Ground speed decreasing
- Bank angle should decrease
- Raise pitch attitude to maintain airspeed
- Briefly advance throttle to normal cruise power to clear engine
- Maintain distance from reference point

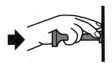

6

- Shallowest bank angle
- Roll out toward a definite object and on a specific heading
- Maintain coordination for a constant airspeed as the straight glide is resumed

Evaluation:

- Select an altitude sufficient to continue through a series of at least three 360° turns
- Select a suitable ground reference point
- Apply wind-drift correction to track a constant radius circle around selected reference point with bank not to exceed 60° at steepest point in turn
- Divide attention between airplane control and ground track, while maintaining coordinated flight
- Maintain airspeed (±10 knots)
- Roll out toward object or specified heading (±10°)

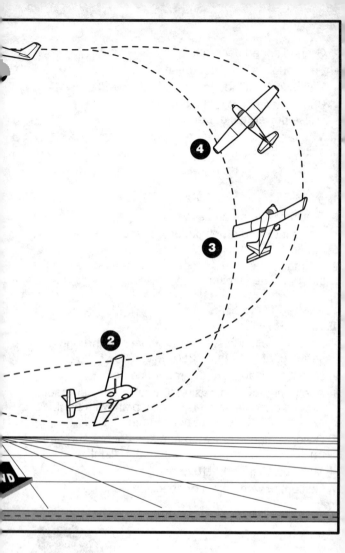

- Pitch airplane up into a climbing turn
- Smoothly apply full power, without exceeding maximum RPM

(continued)

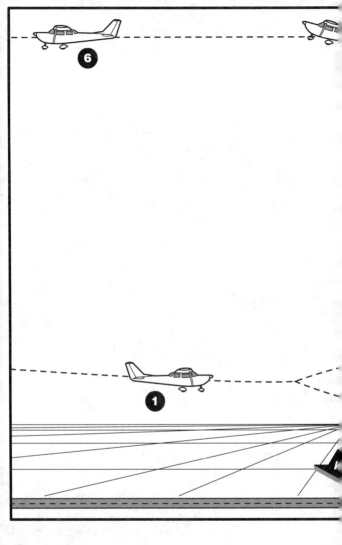

- Roll into the wind, with a 30° bank angle

CHANDELLES

(Commercial, CFI)

Objective: Demonstrate a maximum performance climbing turn, with a heading change of 180°, a maximum gain in altitude, and rolling wings-level just above stall speed.

Task:

- Find practice area where terrain is appropriate for maneuvering, emergency landing area available
- Set power to obtain maneuvering speed (V_A), cruise speed, or manufacturer recommended speed (whichever is less)

  Cruise Speed or Manufacturer Recommended V_A (whichever is less) _____ knots
- Select an altitude that allows maneuver to be performed no lower than 1,500 feet AGL, or manufacturer recommended (whichever is higher)
- Clear area for other aircraft
- Trim airplane for level hands-off flight
- Establish wind direction

DO NOT FORGET CLEARING TURNS

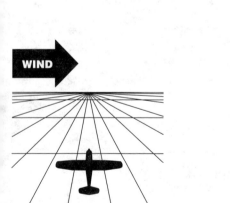

WIND

- Once bank angle is established, neutralize ailerons
- Maintain coordination

- Maintain 30° bank angle until 90°-point
- Continue to increase pitch attitude until 90°-point
- Maintain full power
- Altitude is increasing
- Airspeed is decreasing

- Gradually start rolling out bank at 90°-point
- Maintain pitch attitude
- Maintain coordination

5

- Complete rollout to wings level at 180°-point
- Airspeed is approximately 1.2 V_{S1}, ±5 knots

  1.2 V_{S1} _____ knots

- Momentarily hold airspeed without stalling
- Maintain coordination

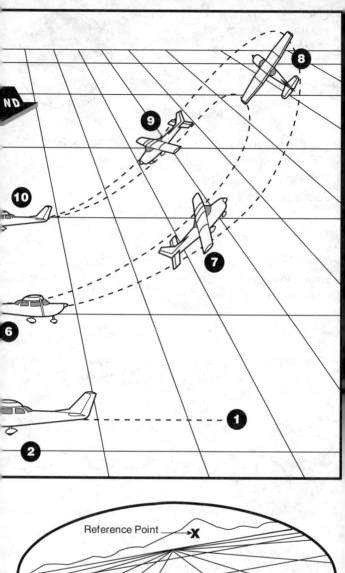

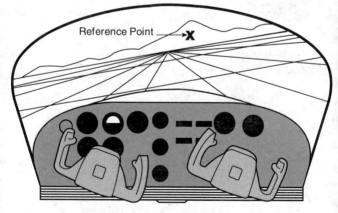

Reference Point → **X**

(continued)

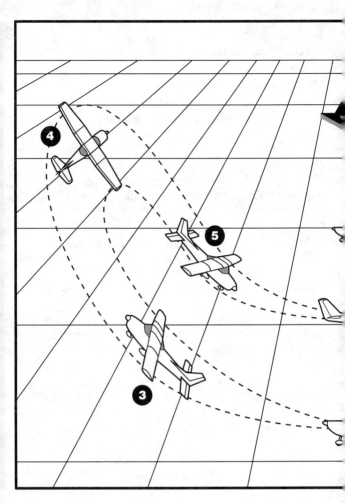

- Pass the 45° reference point with maximum nose-up for maneuver
- Increase bank angle through 15°
- Speed is decreasing
- Pitch attitude begins decreasing
- Bank angle continues to increase

- Resume straight-and-level flight with minimum loss of altitude
- Let airspeed build
- Reduce power to cruise setting
- Repeat maneuver in opposite direction

Evaluation:

- Select an altitude that allows the maneuver to be performed no lower than 1,500 feet AGL or the manufacturer's recommended altitude, whichever is higher
- Establish the entry configuration at an airspeed no greater than the maximum entry speed recommended by the manufacturer (not to exceed V_A)
- Establish approximately, but do not exceed, 30° of bank
- Simultaneously apply specified power and pitch to maintain a smooth, coordinated turn with constant bank to the 90°-point
- Begin a coordinated constant rate of rollout from the 90°-point to the 180°-point maintaining specified power and a constant pitch attitude that will result in a rollout within ±10° of desired heading and airspeed within +5 knots of power-on stall speed
- Reduce pitch attitude to resume straight-and-level flight at the final altitude attained, ±50 feet

LAZY EIGHTS

(Commercial and CFI)

Objective: With constant change in control pressure due to changing combinations of climbing and descending turns at varying airspeeds, experience the full performance range of the airplane while flying a lazy eight pattern.

Task:

- Find practice area where terrain is appropriate for maneuvering, emergency landing area available
- Set power to obtain maneuvering speed (V$_A$), cruise speed, or manufacturer recommended speed (whichever is less)

  Cruise Speed or Manufacturer Recommended V$_A$ (whichever is less) _____ knots
- Select an altitude that allows maneuver to be performed no lower than 1,500 feet AGL, or manufacturer recommended (whichever is higher)
- Clear area for other aircraft
- Trim airplane for level hands-off flight

DO NOT FORGET CLEARING TURNS

- Fly crosswind and select an upwind reference point abeam the wing tip

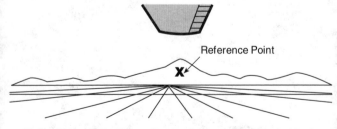

Reference Point

X

- Raise the nose above the horizon and begin a climb
- Slowly roll in bank, and enter a coordinated climbing turn into the wind

4

- Arrive at maximum bank angle 30 at 90° reference point
- Pitch attitude is momentarily level
- Take note of minimum airspeed
- Take note of maximum altitude
- Pitch continues to decrease
- Bank decreases
- Speed increases

5

- Pass the 135° reference point with the lowest nose attitude for the maneuver

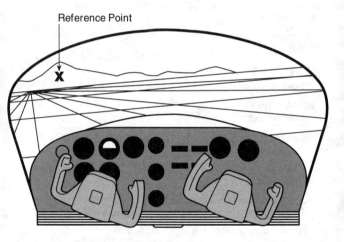

Reference Point

- Reduce bank angle through 15°
- Speed continues to increase
- Pitch begins increasing
- Bank angle continues to decrease

- Look outside, peek inside
- Anticipate the rollout heading or reference point

- Roll out of bank with aileron and coordinated rudder pressure, to return to straight-and-level flight
- Release elevator back pressure

- Repeat the turn in opposite direction
- Exit at point of entry at the same altitude and airspeed at which the maneuver was started
- Adjust power to return to entry airspeed
- Trim to hands-off level flight

Evaluation:

- Establish V_A or the recommended entry speed for the airplane
- Roll into a coordinated 360° turn (45° bank, ±5° for Private and Sport, or 50° bank, ±5° for Commercial)
- Perform the task in the opposite direction
- Roll out on the entry heading (±10° for Private and Sport, ±10° for Commercial)
- Divide attention between airplane control and orientation
- Maintain the entry altitude, ±100 feet, and airspeed (±10 knots for Private and Sport, and ±10 knots for Commercial)

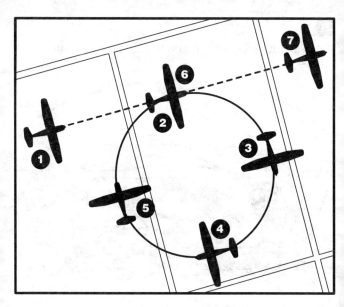

4

- Maintain bank angle with aileron
- Maintain coordination with rudder
- Maintain altitude with elevator, using back pressure on the control column (reference altimeter)
- Trim to maintain altitude (optional)

5

- Add power as required to maintain airspeed
- Apply opposite aileron to prevent overbanking (less correction required for right turns)

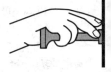

6

- At the 180° reference point, airplane is momentarily level

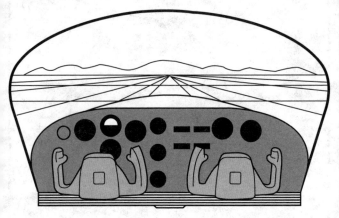

- Altitude is same as entry altitude
- Airspeed is same as entry airspeed
- Begin to raise the nose
- Gently roll bank in the opposite direction

7

- Pass the 45° reference point with maximum nose-up for maneuver
- Increase the bank angle through 15°
- Speed is decreasing
- Pitch attitude begins decreasing
- Bank angle continues to increase

8

- Arrive at maximum bank angle 30° at 90° reference point
- Pitch attitude is momentarily level
- Take note of minimum airspeed
- Take note of maximum altitude
- Pitch continues to decrease
- Bank decreases
- Speed increases

9

- Pass the 135° reference point with the lowest nose attitude for maneuver
- Reduce bank angle through 15°
- Speed continues to increase
- Pitch begins increasing
- Bank angle continues to decrease

10

- At the 180° reference point, airplane is wings-level
- Altitude is same as entry altitude
- Airspeed is same as entry airspeed
- Resume straight-and-level flight

Evaluation:

- Select an altitude that allows the task to be performed no lower than 1,500 feet AGL or the manufacturer's recommended altitude, whichever is higher
- Select a prominent 90° reference point in the distance
- Establish the recommended entry power and airspeed
- Plan to be and remain oriented while maneuvering the airplane with positive, accurate control, and demonstrate mastery of the airplane
- Achieve the following throughout the task—
    a. Constant change of pitch, bank, and turn rate
    b. Altitude and airspeed consistent at the 90°-points, ±100 feet and ±10 knots respectively
    c. Through proper power setting, attain starting altitude and airspeed at the completion of maneuver, ±100 feet and ±10 knots respectively
    d. Heading tolerance ±10° at each 180° point
- Continue task through at least two 180° circuits and resume straight-and-level flight
- Maintain coordination throughout maneuver
- Correct for torque effect in right and left turns
- Loops should be symmetrical
- Pitch and bank attitude should have a constant rate of change throughout the maneuver

STEEP TURNS

(Private, Sport, Commercial, CFI)

Objective: Turn 360° in a steep (more than 45°) bank, maintaining constant altitude and airspeed.

Task: Check Manufacturer Recommendations

- Find practice area where terrain is appropriate for maneuvering, emergency landing area available
- Set power to obtain maneuvering speed (V_A)
  Manufacturer Recommended V_A _____ knots
- Clear area for other aircraft
- Trim airplane for level hands-off flight
- Select a heading or reference point for rollout

DO NOT FORGET CLEARING TURNS

- Look outside, peek inside
- From straight-and-level flight, coordinate aileron and rudder to roll into a 45–50° turn
- Due to torque effect, more rudder is required for right turns
- Exert back pressure on the control column to maintain altitude

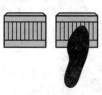

- Look outside, peek inside
- Select a reference point on the horizon to maintain altitude and bank angle

GO-AROUND PROCEDURE

(Private, Sport, Commercial, CFI)

Objective: Discontinue the landing approach in order to make another approach under more favorable conditions.

Task: Check Manufacturer Recommendations

1
- Make a timely decision to discontinue the approach

2
- Apply full takeoff power (throttle full in)

- Adjust the attitude to stop the descent and begin a positive rate of climb
- Carburetor heat off (full in)
- Trim as necessary

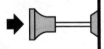

3
- Retract flaps to a takeoff setting once a positive rate of climb is established

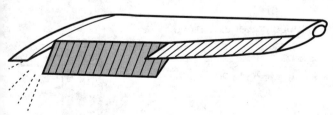

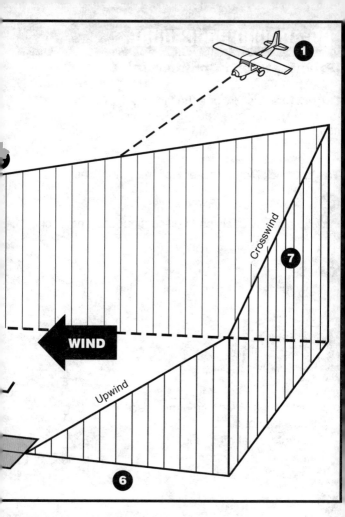

WIND

Crosswind

Upwind

4

- Base leg
- Reduce power to achieve 1.4 V_{S0}
  *Manufacturer Recommended
  1.4 V_{S0} _____ knots*
- Extend flaps to 20°

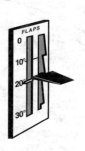

(continued)

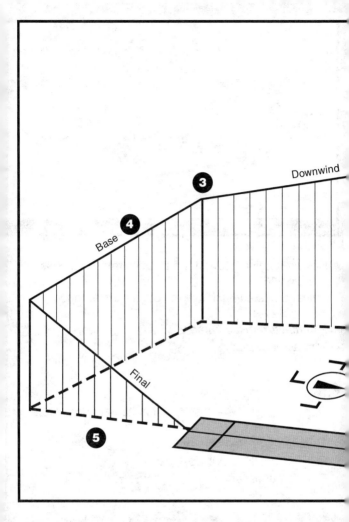

- Abeam the runway numbers, begin descending 400–500 fpm (traffic permitting)
- Coordinate elevator and throttle to control rate of descent and airspeed

3

- Look over shoulder to determine airplane location relative to runway
- At 45° to landing point, begin turn to base leg using a 30° bank angle

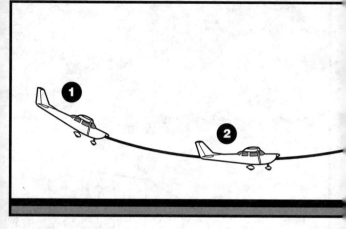

- Retract landing gear after a positive rate of climb is established
- Adjust attitude to achieve the obstacle-clearance airspeed (V_X)
  Manufacturer Recommended V_X _____ knots
- Trim as necessary

- Once clear of obstacles, adjust attitude to accelerate to V_Y
  Manufacturer Recommended V_Y _____ knots
- Fully retract flaps (full up)
- Trim as necessary

- Maneuver to the side of the runway/landing area to clear and avoid conflicting traffic
- Continue in a normal traffic pattern

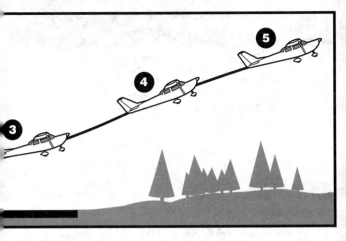

Evaluation:

- Make a timely decision to discontinue the approach to landing
- Apply takeoff power immediately and transition to the climb pitch attitude for V_Y (+10/-5 knots for Private and Sport, ±5 knots for Commercial)
- Retract flaps to the approach setting, if applicable
- Retract landing gear, if retractable, after a positive rate of climb is established
- Maintain takeoff power to a safe maneuvering altitude, then set power and transition to the airspeed appropriate for the traffic pattern
- Maintain directional control and proper wind-drift correction throughout climb
- Comply with noise abatement procedures, as appropriate
- Fly the appropriate traffic pattern
- Complete the appropriate checklist

TRAFFIC PATTERN

(Private, Sport, Commercial, CFI)

Objective: Fly a pattern, designed to assure the orderly flow of arriving and departing air traffic: standard pattern—left turns, nonstandard pattern—right turns.

Task: Check Manufacturer Recommendations

- Complete before-landing checklist
- Determine landing runway (land into the wind)
- Determine direction of traffic pattern (left turns or right turns)
- Obtain clearance or advise traffic of position and intentions
- Enter traffic pattern at a 45° angle to the downwind, at traffic pattern altitude (usually 800–1,000 feet AGL)
  Traffic Pattern Altitude _____ feet MSL

- Downwind leg
- Reduce power to achieve 1.5 V_{S0}
  Manufacturer Recommended 1.5 V_{S0} _____ knots
- Pull carburetor heat on (fully out) as required
- Maintain traffic pattern altitude and 1/2–1 mile out from landing runway
- Extend flaps to 10°, then within the white arc of airspeed indicator

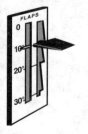

- Continue descending 400–500 fpm
- Coordinate elevator and throttle to control rate of descent and airspeed
- Begin turn to final in order to arrive on extended runway centerline, using a 20° bank angle
- Complete turn to final 1/4 mile from runway

- Final leg
- Align with runway centerline
- Select landing flaps

- Lower the nose to maintain 1.3 V_{S0} or approach speed
  Manufacturer Recommended 1.3 V_{S0} or approach speed _____ *knots*
- Coordinate elevator and throttle to control rate of descent and airspeed
- Crossing runway threshold, pull throttle to idle
- Touchdown first 1/4 of runway

- Upwind leg
- Fly out on extended runway centerline until reaching a point beyond the departure end of runway and within 300 feet of traffic pattern altitude

- Maintain bank angle with aileron—the steeper the bank angle, the faster the rate of descent
- Maintain flight path with opposite rudder
- Maintain airspeed with elevator (airspeed indicator may be inaccurate in this configuration)

- Remove the forward slip with enough altitude for safe recovery
- Level the wings with aileron
- Remove opposite rudder and resume coordinated flight, keeping aligned with runway
- Maintain desired airspeed with elevator
- Assume normal glide before touchdown

Evaluation:

- Consider the wind conditions, landing surface and obstructions, and select the most suitable touchdown point
- Establish slipping attitude at the point from which a landing can be made using the recommended approach and landing configuration and airspeed; adjust the pitch attitude and power as required
- Maintain a ground track aligned with the runway centerline and an airspeed that results in minimum float during the roundout
- Make smooth, timely, and correct control application during the recovery from the slip, the roundout, and the touchdown
- Touch down smoothly at the appropriate stalling speed, at or within 400 feet beyond a specified point, with no side drift, and with the airplane's longitudinal axis aligned with and over runway centerline
- Maintain crosswind correction and directional control throughout approach and landing
- Complete the appropriate checklist

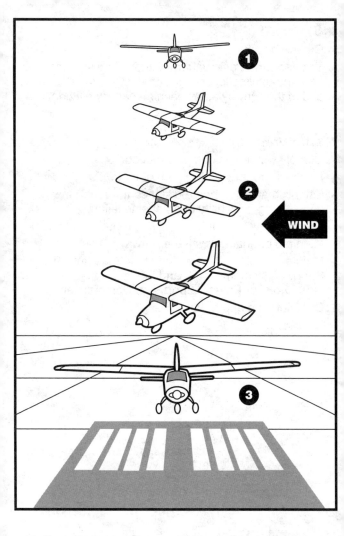

- Maintain flight path with opposite rudder (uncoordinated flight)

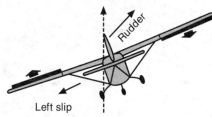

- Hold nose attitude and maintain airspeed with elevator

- Crosswind leg
- To depart the traffic pattern, either climb straight out from the upwind leg, or turn 45° beyond the departure end of the runway after reaching pattern altitude

Evaluation:

- Comply with traffic pattern procedures
- Maintain proper spacing from other traffic
- Establish an appropriate distance from the runway, considering possibility of an engine failure
- Correct for wind drift to maintain proper ground track
- Maintain orientation with the runway in use
- Maintain traffic pattern altitude (±100 feet for Private, Sport, and Commercial), and the appropriate airspeed (±10 knots for Private, Sport, and Commercial)
- Complete the appropriate checklist

FORWARD SLIP

(Private, Sport, CFI)

Objective: Dissipate altitude by increasing the rate of descent, and steepen the descent flight path without increasing airspeed by forward slipping using crossed-controls.

Task: Check Manufacturer Recommendations

- Position airplane too high on final approach in a normal glide
- Follow manufacturer recommendations for use of flaps during a slip
- Reduce power to IDLE (full out)

- Carburetor heat on (full out)

- Establish slightly less than a normal glide speed
  Manufacturer Recommended glide speed _____ knots

- Apply bank in the direction of slip with aileron control (slip into the wind)

NORMAL APPROACH & LANDING

(Private, Sport, Commercial, CFI)

Objective: Make a normal approach and transition the airplane from the air to the ground, landing into a headwind.

Task: Check Manufacturer Recommendations

- Complete a normal traffic pattern (see Page 42)
- Final approach, align with runway centerline
- Select landing flaps

- Verify landing gear down
- Lower the nose to maintain 1.3 V_{S0} or approach speed
  Manufacturer Recommended approach speed or 1.3 V_{S0} _____ knots
- **Fly**—coordinate elevator and throttle to control rate of descent and airspeed
- Maintain constant descent rate

- **Float**—reduce power to IDLE (throttle fully out)
- Descent rate slows

3

- **Flare**—stop the descent rate by beginning to pull back on elevator
- Progressively raise the nose to hold airplane off just above runway as airspeed slows to approximately stalling speed
- Hold upwind wing down, maintaining track down runway with opposite rudder

4

- **Touchdown**—transiti`on the weight of airplane from the wings to the wheels
- Touchdown on upwind main wheel first, followed by downwind main wheel
- Keep straight with rudder, and hold full aileron into the wind
- Gently lower nose wheel to the runway
- Use brakes to stop and clear runway
- Complete after-landing check (see Page 52)

Evaluation:

- Consider the wind conditions, landing surface and obstructions, and select the most suitable touchdown point
- Establish the recommended approach and landing configuration and airspeed, and adjust pitch attitude and power as required
- Maintain a stabilized approach and the recommended approach airspeed, or in its absence, not more than $1.3\ V_{S0}$ (+10/-5 knots for Private and Sport, ±5 knots for Commercial) with gust factor applied
- Make smooth, timely, and correct control application during the roundout and touchdown
- Touch down smoothly at the approximate stalling speed (at or within 400 feet for Private and Sport, at or within 200 feet for Commercial) beyond a specified point, with no drift, and with the airplane's longitudinal axis aligned with and over the runway centerline
- Maintain crosswind correction and directional control throughout the approach and landing
- Complete the appropriate checklist

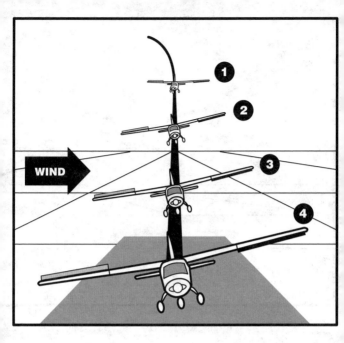

2

- **Float**—reduce power to IDLE (throttle fully out)
- Descent rate slows
- Remove crab angle
- Lower the upwind wing
- Maintain track down extended runway with opposite rudder

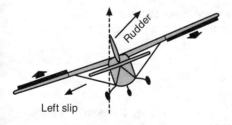

Rudder

Left slip

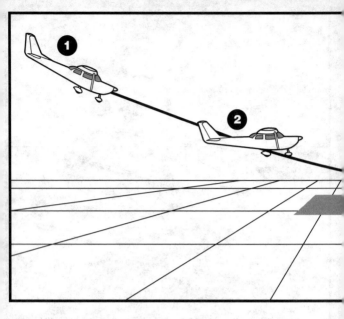

Flare—stop the descent rate by beginning to pull back on elevator

- Progressively raise the nose to hold airplane off just above runway as airspeed slows to approximately stalling speed

- **Touchdown**—transition the weight of airplane from the wings to the wheels
- Touchdown on the main wheels first and hold nose-wheel off with back elevator pressure
- Keep straight with rudder, and wings level with aileron
- Gently lower nose wheel to runway
- Use brakes to stop and clear runway
- Complete after-landing check (see Page 52)

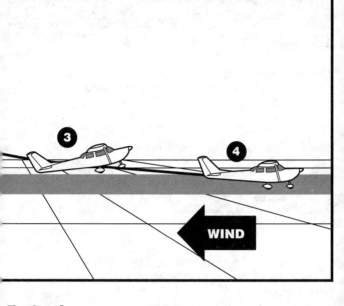

Evaluation:

- Consider the wind conditions, landing surface and obstructions, and select the most suitable touchdown point
- Establish the recommended approach and landing configuration and airspeed, and adjust pitch attitude and power as required
- Maintain a stabilized approach and the recommended approach airspeed, or in its absence, not more than $1.3\ V_{S0}$ (+10/-5 knots for Private and Sport, ±5 knots for Commercial) with gust factor applied
- Make smooth, timely, and correct control application during the roundout and touchdown
- Touch down smoothly at the approximate stalling speed (at or within 400 feet for Private and Sport, at or within 200 feet for Commercial) beyond a specified point, with no drift, and with the airplane's longitudinal axis aligned with and over the runway centerline
- Maintain crosswind correction and directional control throughout the approach and landing
- Complete the appropriate checklist

CROSSWIND APPROACH & LANDING

(Private, Sport, Commercial, CFI)

Objective: Make a crosswind approach and transition the airplane from the air to the ground, landing with a crosswind, using both the crab and wing-low method.

Task: Check Manufacturer Recommendations

- Complete a normal traffic pattern (see Page 42)
- Verify crosswind component will not be exceeded
  Manufacturer Recommended Crosswind Component _____ knots
- Final approach, track down extended runway center-line by heading airplane into the wind (apply a wind correction angle)

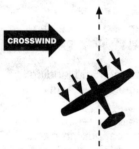

- The wings should be level, except when adjusting crab angle
- Maintain coordinated flight
- Select landing flaps
- Verify landing gear down
- Lower the nose to maintain 1.3 V_{S0} or approach speed
  Manufacturer Recommended approach speed or 1.3 V_{S0} _____ knots
- **Fly**—coordinate elevator and throttle to control rate of descent and airspeed
- Maintain constant descent rate

SOFT-FIELD APPROACH & LANDING

(Private, Sport, Commercial, CFI)

Objective: Land as slowly as possible, and hold the nose wheel clear of the surface as long as possible.

Task: Check Manufacturer Recommendations

- Complete a normal traffic pattern (see Page 42)
- Final approach, align with runway centerline
- Select landing flaps

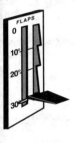

- Verify landing gear down
- Lower the nose to maintain 1.3 V_{S0} or approach speed
  Manufacturer Recommended approach speed or 1.3 V_{S0} _____ knots
- **Fly**—coordinate elevator and throttle to control rate of descent and airspeed
- Maintain constant descent rate

- **Float**—reduce power to IDLE (throttle fully out)
- Descent rate slows

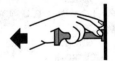

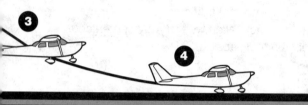

Evaluation:

- Consider the wind conditions, landing surface and obstructions, and select the most suitable touchdown point
- Establish the recommended approach and landing configuration and airspeed, and adjust pitch attitude and power as required
- Maintain a stabilized approach and the recommended approach airspeed, or in its absence not more than 1.3 V_{S0} (+10/-5 knots for Private and Sport, ±5 knots for Commercial), with gust factor applied
- Make smooth, timely, and correct control application during the roundout and touchdown
- Touch down smoothly at the approximate stalling speed, (at or within 200 feet for Private and Sport, at or within 100 feet for Commercial) beyond a specified point, with no side drift, and with the airplane's longitudinal axis aligned with and over the runway centerline
- Apply brakes, as necessary, to stop in the shortest distance consistent with safety
- Maintain crosswind correction and directional control throughout the approach and landing
- Complete the appropriate checklist

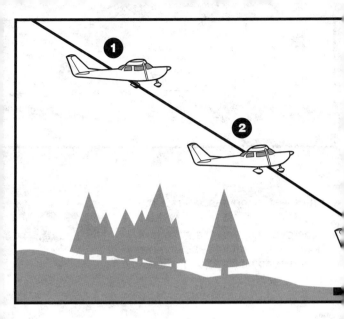

4

- Reduce power to IDLE (throttle fully out)
- **Touchdown**—transition the weight of airplane from the wings to the wheels
- Touchdown with minimum floating, on main wheels first and hold nose wheel off with back elevator pressure
- Keep straight with rudder, and wings level with aileron
- Gently lower nose wheel to runway
- Apply brakes to stop in the shortest possible distance consistent with safety

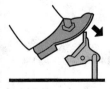

- Complete after-landing check (see Page 52)

3

- **Flare**—stop the descent rate by starting to pull back on elevator
- Progressively raise the nose to hold airplane off just above runway as airspeed slows to approximately stalling speed

4

- **Touchdown**—transition the weight of airplane from the wings to the wheels at the slowest possible speed
- Touchdown on main wheels first and hold nose wheel off with back elevator pressure and power
- Keep straight with rudder, and wings level with aileron

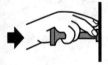

5

- Gently lower nose wheel to runway
- Use power and keep airplane moving in order to taxi without getting stuck in the soft surface
- Avoid using brakes to prevent excessive loads on nose gear
- Complete after-landing check (see Page 52)

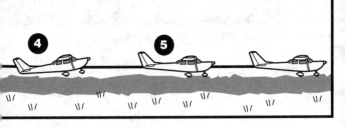

Evaluation:

- Consider the wind conditions, landing surface and obstructions, and select the most suitable touchdown point
- Establish the recommended approach and landing configuration and airspeed, and adjust pitch attitude and power as required
- Maintain a stabilized approach and the recommended approach airspeed, or in its absence not more than 1.3 V_{S0} (+10/-5 knots for Private and Sport, ±5 knots for Commercial), with gust factor applied
- Make smooth, timely, and correct control application during the roundout and touchdown
- Touch down smoothly with no drift, and with the airplane's longitudinal axis aligned with and over the runway centerline
- Maintain the correct position of the flight controls and sufficient speed to taxi on soft surface
- Maintain crosswind correction and directional control throughout approach and landing
- Complete the appropriate checklist

SHORT-FIELD APPROACH & LANDING

(Private, Sport, Commercial, CFI)

Objective: Fly over an obstacle at the approach end of the runway, touch down and stop in the shortest possible distance, at the minimum speed.

Task: Check Manufacturer Recommendations

- Complete a normal traffic pattern (see Page 42)
- Final approach, align with runway centerline
- Select landing flaps
- Verify landing gear down
- Lower the nose to maintain 1.3 V_{S0} or short-field approach speed

  Manufacturer Recommended short-field approach speed or 1.3 V_{S0} _____ knots
- **Fly**—coordinate elevator and throttle to control rate of descent and airspeed
- Maintain constant descent rate to clear all obstacles

- **Float**—reduce power
- Descent rate slows

- **Flare**—stop the descent rate by starting to pull back on elevator
- Since the nose will be higher than a normal approach (because of the lower speed and higher power), less flare is needed and should be started closer to the ground than normal
- Progressively raise the nose to hold the airplane off just above runway as airspeed slows to approximately stalling speed

POWER-OFF 180° ACCURACY APPROACH & LANDING

(Commercial, CFI)

Objective: Develop judgment in estimating distances and glide ratios, flying the airplane without power from a higher altitude and through two 90° turns to execute a safe approach and landing.

Task: Check Manufacturer Recommendations

- Line airplane up on downwind, heading parallel to the landing runway
- Extend landing gear (if retractable)
- Altitude should not exceed 1,000 feet AGL

2

- Close throttle
- Maintain altitude
- Establish glide speed
  Manufacturer Recommended best glide speed _____ knots
- Trim airplane
- Apply carburetor heat
- Mixture rich
- Primer in and locked

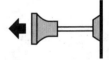

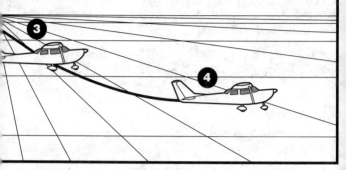

Evaluation:

- Recognize situations, such as depressurization, cockpit smoke, and/or fire that require an emergency descent
- Establish the appropriate airspeed (±10 knots for Commercial) and configuration for the emergency descent
- Exhibit orientation, division of attention, and proper planning
- Maintain positive load factors during the descent
- Commercial: maintain appropriate airspeed, +0/-10 knots, and level off at specified altitude, ±100 feet
- Complete appropriate checklists

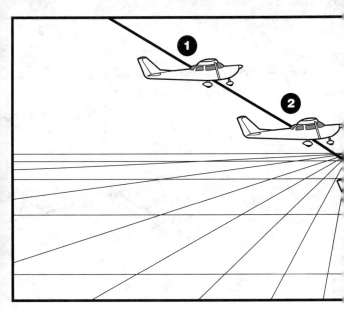

3

- Descend at maximum allowable airspeed
- Do not exceed V_{NE}, V_{LE}, or V_{FE}
- Do not exceed V_A if turbulent

4

- After established and stabilized descent, terminate descent
- Avoid prolonged practice to prevent excessive cooling of the engine cylinders

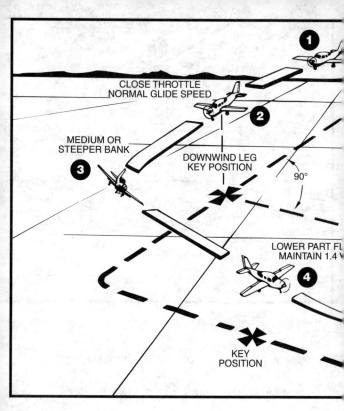

CLOSE THROTTLE
NORMAL GLIDE SPEED

MEDIUM OR
STEEPER BANK

DOWNWIND LEG
KEY POSITION

90°

LOWER PART FL
MAINTAIN 1.4 V

KEY
POSITION

3

- Medium or slightly steeper bank
- Dissipate altitude for normal approach

4

- Lower flaps, as required
- Maintain glide speed
- Execute before landing checklist

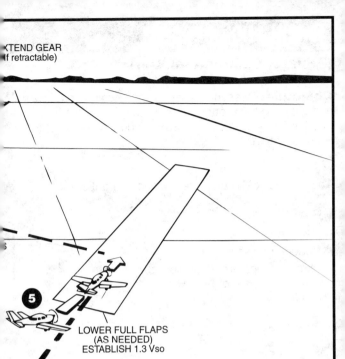

EXTEND GEAR
(if retractable)

LOWER FULL FLAPS
(AS NEEDED)
ESTABLISH 1.3 Vso

5

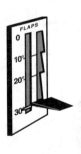

- Lower full flaps, as needed
- Establish 1.3 V_{S0}

Evaluation:

- Consider the wind conditions, landing surface, obstructions, and select an appropriate touchdown point
- Position airplane on downwind leg, parallel to landing runway, and not more than 1,000 feet AGL
- Abeam the specified touchdown point, close throttle and establishes appropriate glide speed
- Complete final airplane configuration
- Touch down in a normal landing attitude, at or within 200 feet beyond the specified touchdown point
- Complete the appropriate checklist

EMERGENCY DESCENT

(Private, Commercial, CFI)

Objective: Descend as rapidly as possible to a lower altitude or to the ground for an emergency situation, such as an uncontrollable fire or sudden loss of cabin pressurization.

Task: Check Manufacturer Recommendations

- Recognize emergency situation
- Reduce power to idle
- Place prop control (if equipped) in the low pitch (or high RPM) position

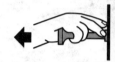

- Extend landing gear
- Extend flaps as recommended by the manufacturer

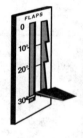

EMERGENCY APPROACH & LANDING

(Private, Commercial, CFI)

Objective: Execute a safe approach and landing following engine failure.

Task: Check Manufacturer Recommendations

- Recognize emergency situation
- Convert excess speed to distance or altitude
- Establish best glide speed
  Manufacturer Recommended best glide speed _____ knots
- Trim airplane
- Determine wind direction
- Select a landing area within gliding range
- Keep all turns toward the selected area

- Time permitting, try to determine cause of failure
- Check fuel selector is set to proper tank
- Apply carburetor heat

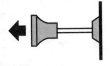

- Try operating magneto on Right, Left, or Both
- Mixture to RICH (fully in)
- Primer in and locked

- Master switch OFF

- Install control lock
- Secure the seatbelts and shoulder harnesses

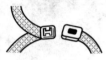

- Record the engine (or Hobbs) time in the log
- Install wheel chock
- Tie down airplane
- Release parking brake
- Install pitot cover
- Refuel airplane
- Perform a brief walk-around inspection of airplane
- Lock doors and return the key
- Report any problem or defects with airplane
- Complete logbook

- Cowl flaps OPEN (if equipped)
- Park airplane into expected wind
- Set parking brake

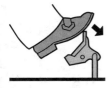

- Throttle to IDLE

- Propeller control (if equipped) to high RPM
- All electrical switches OFF
- Mixture IDLE (fully out)
- Magnetos/Ignition switch OFF after propeller stops

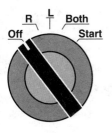

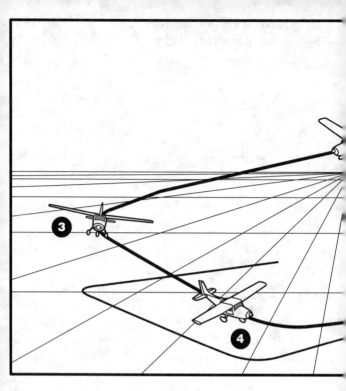

③

- If engine cannot be restarted, execute emergency landing checklist
- Fasten seat belts
- Mixture to IDLE (fully out)
- Fuel selector OFF
- Ignition switch OFF
- Squawk 7700 on transponder
- Tune radio to 121.5 and declare intentions
- Master switch OFF

④

- Check field size, terrain, and obstructions
- Keep field in sight at all times
- Use flaps as required
- If too high, apply a slip

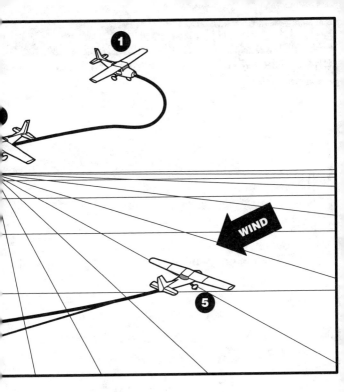

- Unlatch doors prior to touchdown
- Touch down as slow as possible, in a full-stall attitude
- Hold yoke fully back, to keep nose wheel off the ground as long as possible

Evaluation:

- Establish and maintain the recommended best-glide attitude, configuration, and airspeed (±10 knots for Private and Commercial)
- Select a suitable emergency landing area within gliding distance
- Plan and follow a flight pattern to the selected landing area considering altitude, wind, terrain, and obstructions
- Attempt to determine reason for the malfunction and make the correction, if possible
- Maintain positive control of the airplane at all times
- Follow the appropriate emergency checklist

AFTER-LANDING CHECK

Check Manufacturer Recommendations

- Clear runway
- Flaps, fully up

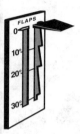

- Carburetor heat OFF (fully in)

- Taxi to parking area, using proper wind control technique

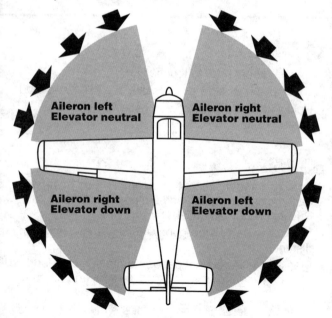

**Aileron left
Elevator neutral**

**Aileron right
Elevator neutral**

**Aileron right
Elevator down**

**Aileron left
Elevator down**

 Indicated Wind Direction Taxiing

ENERGY MANAGEMENT GUIDE

Energy Management Definition

Energy management is the process of planning, monitoring, and controlling altitude and airspeed targets in relation to the airplane's energy state in order to:

1. Attain and maintain desired vertical flightpath-airspeed profiles.

2. Detect, correct, and prevent unintentional altitude-airspeed deviations from the desired energy state.

3. Prevent irreversible deceleration and/or sink rate that results in a crash.

Energy Balance Equation

$$\left(\begin{array}{c}\text{Energy} \\ \text{gained from} \\ \text{thrust (T)}\end{array}\right) - \left(\begin{array}{c}\text{Energy} \\ \text{lost through} \\ \text{drag (D)}\end{array}\right) = \left(\begin{array}{c}\text{Change in} \\ \text{potential} \\ \text{energy}\end{array}\right) + \left(\begin{array}{c}\text{Change in} \\ \text{kinetic} \\ \text{energy}\end{array}\right)$$

| **Energy In** | **Energy Out** | **Altitude Change** | **Airspeed Change** |

Net Energy Change = Change in Stored Energy

Roles of the Flight Controls

Throttle = Total Energy Controller

Once a desired path–speed profile is established, the throttle will set the engine thrust to match the total energy demanded by the vertical flight path and airspeed combined.

Elevator = Energy Distribution Controller

Once a desired path–speed profile is achieved, the elevator sets the appropriate pitch attitude to maintain the demanded distribution of total energy over vertical flight path and airspeed.

energy state.

State Matrix.

d Speed	Faster
ing to reduce total r to maintain correct he airplane to	(7) Reduce throttle setting significantly to decrease total energy. Pull back on elevator gradually to decelerate to correct airspeed and then descend.
State e and elevator (trim)	(8) Reduce throttle setting to decelerate. Use elevator to maintain the desired altitude.
ting to gain altitude vator to maintain	(9) Exchange energy by pulling the elevator back to climb and decelerate simultaneously. Maintain the throttle setting.

needed to maintain a constant pitch attitude.

...de–speed deviations into energy errors relative to the desire...

...y State Matrix

...irspeed		
Desired Airspeed		**Faster**
(4) Total energy: high Potential energy: high Kinetic energy: OK		(7) Total energy: very high Potential energy: high Kinetic energy: high
(5) Desired Energy State Total energy: OK Potential energy: OK Kinetic energy: OK		(8) Total energy: high Potential energy: OK Kinetic energy: high
(6) Total energy: low Potential energy: low Kinetic energy: OK		(9) Total energy: OK Potential energy: low Kinetic energy: high

...tal energy and energy distribution errors identified in the Ene...

Control Skills to Correct Energy Errors

	Airspeed	
	Slower	**Des...**
...g the	(1) Exchange energy by pushing the elevator forward to accelerate and descend simultaneously. Maintain the throttle setting.	(4) Reduce throttle energy. Use elev... airspeed and all... descend.
...he ...o ...ll	(2) Increase throttle setting to gain total energy by accelerating. Use elevator to maintain the desired altitude.	**(5) Desired Ene...** Maintain both th... settings.
...solve ...hich ...r ...on the ...rve.*	(3) Increase throttle setting significantly to gain total energy. Push elevator forward gradually to accelerate to correct airspeed and then climb.	(6) Increase throttle and pull back or... correct airspeed

...rt of the correction maneuver, slight forward or aft elevator pressure ma...
...ate to correct airspeed and then climb.

Rules of Energy Control

Rule #1: If you want to move to a new energy state that demands more total energy, then:

- **Throttle:** Increase throttle setting so that thrust is greater than drag, thus increasing total energy;
- **Elevator:** Adjust pitch attitude as appropriate to distribute the total energy being gained over altitude and airspeed:
  a. To climb at constant speed, pitch up just enough to maintain the desired speed.
  b. To accelerate at constant altitude, gradually pitch down just enough to maintain path.

Upon reaching the new desired energy state, adjust pitch attitude and throttle setting as needed to maintain the new path–speed profile.

Rule #2: If you want to move to a new energy state that demands less total energy, then:

- **Throttle:** Reduce throttle setting so that thrust is less than drag, thus decreasing total energy;
- **Elevator:** Adjust pitch attitude as appropriate to distribute the total energy being lost over altitude and airspeed:
  a. To descend at constant speed, pitch down just enough to maintain the desired speed.
  b. To slow down at constant altitude, gradually pitch up just enough to maintain path.

Upon reaching the new desired energy state, adjust pitch attitude and throttle setting as needed to maintain the new path–speed profile.

Rule #3: If you want to move to a new energy state that demands no change in total energy, then:

- **Throttle:** Do not change initially, but adjust it to match drag at the end of the maneuver as needed to maintain total energy constant;
- **Elevator:** Adjust pitch attitude to exchange energy between altitude and airspeed:
  a. To trade speed for altitude, pitch up.
  b. To trade altitude for speed, pitch down.

Upon reaching the new desired energy state, adjust pitch attitude and throttle setting as needed to maintain the new path–speed profile.

(continued)

Energy Error Management

Below is an energy-state matrix that translates the main a▮

Ene▮

		Slower
Altitude	**Higher**	(1) Total energy: OK Potential energy: high Kinetic energy: low
	Desired Altitude	(2) Total energy: low Potential energy: OK Kinetic energy: low
	Lower	(3) Total energy: very low Potential energy: low Kinetic energy: low

The table below shows the control skills needed to correct

		Cautions When Very Sl▮
Altitude	**Higher**	Relatively safe. Surplus altitude available to gain speed by push▮ elevator forward.
	Desired Altitude	Risky. Consider gaining speed ▮ expense of some altitude initiall▮ improve climb performance with▮ throttle.
	Lower	Dangerous! Apply full throttle to▮ this condition. Avoid pitching up▮ would increase drag and reduce▮ impede climb performance whe▮ backside of the power required▮

* Depending on aircraft type, as full throttle is applied at the s▮
As the airplane gains total energy, use the elevator to accel▮

PRIVATE CHECKLIST

Private Pilot Airman Certification Standards Checklist (ASEL)

I.   Preflight Preparation
- ❑ A. Pilot Qualifications
- ❑ B. Airworthiness Requirements
- ❑ C. Weather Information
- ❑ D. Cross-Country Flight Planning
- ❑ E. National Airspace System
- ❑ F. Performance and Limitations
- ❑ G. Operation of Systems
- ❑ H. Human Factors

II.   Preflight Procedures
- ❑ A. Preflight Assessment
- ❑ B. Cockpit Management
- ❑ C. Engine Starting
- ❑ D. Taxiing
- ❑ F. Before Takeoff Check

III. Airport Operations
- ❑ A. Communications and Light Gun Signals
- ❑ B. Traffic Patterns

IV.   Takeoffs, Landing and Go-arounds
- ❑ A. Normal Takeoff and Climb
- ❑ B. Normal Approach and Landing
- ❑ C. Soft-Field Takeoff and Climb
- ❑ D. Soft-Field Approach and Landing
- ❑ E. Short-Field Takeoff and Maximum Performance Climb
- ❑ F. Short-Field Approach and Landing
- ❑ M. Forward Slip to a Landing
- ❑ N. Go-Around/Rejected Landing

V.   Performance Maneuvers
- ❑ A. Steep Turns
- ❑ B. Ground Reference Maneuvers

V. Performance Maneuver
- ❏ A. Steep turns

VI. Ground Reference Maneuvers
- ❏ A. Rectangular course
- ❏ B. S-turns
- ❏ C. Turns around a point

VII. Navigation
- ❏ A. Pilotage and dead reckoning
- ❏ B. Diversion
- ❏ C. Lost procedures

VIII. Slow flight and stalls
- ❏ A. Maneuvering during slow flight
- ❏ B. Power-off stalls
- ❏ C. Power-on stalls
- ❏ D. Spin awareness

IX. Emergency operations
- ❏ A. Emergency approach and landing
- ❏ B. Systems and equipment malfunctions
- ❏ C. Emergency equipment and survival gear

X. Postflight procedures
- ❏ A. After landing, parking and securing

VI. Navigation
- ❑ A. Pilotage and Dead Reckoning
- ❑ B. Navigation Systems and Radar Services
- ❑ C. Diversion
- ❑ D. Lost Procedures

VII. Slow Flight and Stalls
- ❑ A. Maneuvering During Slow Flight
- ❑ B. Power-Off stalls
- ❑ C. Power-On Stalls
- ❑ D. Spin Awareness

VIII. Basic Instrument Maneuvers
- ❑ A. Straight-and-Level Flight
- ❑ B. Constant Airspeed Climbs
- ❑ C. Constant Airspeed Descents
- ❑ D. Turns to Headings
- ❑ E. Recovery from Unusual Flight Attitudes
- ❑ F. Radio Communications, Navigation Systems/ Facilities, and Radar Services

IX. Emergency Operations
- ❑ A. Emergency Descent
- ❑ B. Emergency Approach and Landing (Simulated)
- ❑ C. Systems and Equipment Malfunction
- ❑ D. Emergency Equipment and Survival Gear
- ❑ E. Engine Failure During Takeoff Before V_{MC} (Simulated)
- ❑ F. Engine Failure After Lift-Off (Simulated)
- ❑ G. Approach and Landing with an Inoperative Engine (Simulated)

XI. Night Operations
- ❑ A. Night Preparation

XII. Postflight Procedures
- ❑ A. After Landing, Parking and Securing

SPORT CHECKLIST

Sport Practical Test Standards Checklist (ASEL)

I. Preflight Preparation
- ❏ A. Certificates and documents
- ❏ B. Airworthiness requirements
- ❏ C. Weather information
- ❏ D. Cross-country flight planning
- ❏ E. National airspace system
- ❏ F. Operation of systems
- ❏ G. Aeromedical factors
- ❏ H. Performance and limitations
- ❏ I. Principles of flight

II. Preflight Procedures
- ❏ A. Preflight inspection
- ❏ B. Cockpit management
- ❏ C. Engine starting
- ❏ D. Taxiing
- ❏ E. Before takeoff check

III. Airport Operations
- ❏ A. Radio communications
- ❏ B. Traffic patterns
- ❏ C. Airport, runway, taxiway signs, markings and lighting

IV. Takeoffs, Landings, and Go-Arounds
- ❏ A. Normal and crosswind takeoff and climb
- ❏ B. Normal and crosswind approach and landing
- ❏ C. Soft-field takeoff and climb
- ❏ D. Soft-field approach and landing
- ❏ E. Short-field takeoff and climb
- ❏ F. Short-field approach and landing
- ❏ G. Go-around/Rejected landing

COMMERCIAL CHECKLIST

Commercial Practical Test Standards Checklist (ASEL)

I.   Preflight Preparation
- ❑ A. Certificates and documents
- ❑ B. Airworthiness requirements
- ❑ C. Weather information
- ❑ D. Cross-country flight planning
- ❑ E. National airspace system
- ❑ F. Performance and limitations
- ❑ G. Operation of systems
- ❑ H. Aeromedical factors

II.   Preflight Procedures
- ❑ A. Preflight inspection
- ❑ B. Cockpit management
- ❑ C. Engine starting
- ❑ D. Taxiing
- ❑ E. Runway incursion avoidance
- ❑ F. Before-takeoff check

III.   Airport Operations
- ❑ A. Radio communications and ATC light signals
- ❑ B. Traffic patterns
- ❑ C. Airport, runway, and taxiway signs, markings, and lighting

IV.   Takeoffs, Landings, and Go-arounds
- ❑ A. Normal and crosswind takeoff and climb
- ❑ B. Normal and crosswind approach and landing
- ❑ C. Soft-field takeoff and climb
- ❑ D. Soft-field approach and landing
- ❑ E. Short-field takeoff and climb
- ❑ F. Short-field approach and landing
- ❑ G. Power-off 180° accuracy approach and landing
- ❑ H. Go-around/Rejected landing

IX.   Performance Maneuvers
- ❏   A.   Steep turns
- ❏   B.   Steep spirals
- ❏   C.   Chandelles
- ❏   D.   Lazy eights

X.   Ground Reference Maneuvers
- ❏   A.   Rectangular course
- ❏   B.   S-turns across a road
- ❏   C.   Turns around a point
- ❏   D.   Eights-on-pylons

XI.   Slow Flight, Stalls, and Spins
- ❏   A.   Maneuvering during slow flight
- ❏   B.   Power-on stalls
- ❏   C.   Power-off stalls
- ❏   D.   Cross-controlled stalls
- ❏   E.   Elevator trim stalls
- ❏   F.   Secondary stalls
- ❏   G.   Spins
- ❏   H.   Accelerated maneuver stalls

XII.   Basic Instrument Maneuvers
- ❏   A.   Straight-and-level flight
- ❏   B.   Constant airspeed climbs
- ❏   C.   Constant airspeed descents
- ❏   D.   Turns to headings
- ❏   E.   Recovery from unusual attitudes

XIII.   Emergency Operations
- ❏   A.   Emergency approach and landing (simulated)
- ❏   B.   Systems and equipment malfunctions
- ❏   C.   Emergency equipment and survival gear
- ❏   D.   Emergency descent

XIV.   Postflight Procedures
- ❏   A.   Postflight procedures

IV. Preflight Lesson on a Maneuver to be Performed in Flight
❑ Maneuver lesson

V. Preflight Procedures
❑ A. Preflight inspection
❑ B. Cockpit management
❑ C. Engine starting
❑ D. Taxiing—landplane
❑ E. Before takeoff check

VI. Airport Operations
❑ A. Radio communications and ATC light signals
❑ B. Traffic patterns
❑ C. Airport, runway, and taxiway signs, markings, and lighting

VII. Takeoffs, Landings, and Go-Arounds
❑ A. Normal and crosswind takeoff and climb
❑ B. Short-field takeoff and maximum performance climb
❑ C. Soft-field takeoff and climb
❑ D. Normal and crosswind approach and landing
❑ E. Slip to a landing
❑ F. Go-Around/Rejected landing
❑ G. Short-field approach and landing
❑ H. Soft-field approach and landing
❑ I. Power-off 180° accuracy approach and landing

VIII. Fundamentals of Flight
❑ A. Straight-and-level flight
❑ B. Level turns
❑ C. Straight climbs and climbing turns
❑ D. Straight descents and descending turns

V.   Performance Maneuvers
☐   A.   Steep turns
☐   B.   Steep spirals
☐   C.   Chandelles
☐   D.   Lazy eights

VI.   Ground Reference Maneuver
☐   Eights-on-pylons

VII.   Navigation
☐   A.   Pilotage and dead reckoning
☐   B.   Navigation systems and ATC radar services
☐   C.   Diversion
☐   D.   Lost procedures

VIII. Slow Flight and Stalls
☐   A.   Maneuvering during slow flight
☐   B.   Power-off stalls
☐   C.   Power-on stalls
☐   D.   Accelerated stalls
☐   E.   Spin awareness

IX.   Emergency Operations
☐   A.   Emergency descent
☐   B.   Emergency approach and landing
☐   C.   Systems and equipment malfunctions
☐   D.   Emergency equipment and survival gear

X.   High Altitude Operations
☐   A.   Supplemental Oxygen
☐   B.   Pressurization

XI.   Postflight Procedures
☐   A.   After-landing
☐   B.   Parking and securing

FLIGHT INSTRUCTOR CHECKLIST

Flight Instructor Practical Test Standards Checklist (ASEL)

I. Fundamentals of Instructing
- ❏ A. Human behavior and effective communication
- ❏ B. The learning process
- ❏ C. The teaching process
- ❏ D. Assessment and critique
- ❏ E. Instructor responsibilities and professionalism
- ❏ F. Techniques of flight instruction
- ❏ G. Risk management

II. Technical Subject Areas
- ❏ A. Aeromedical factors
- ❏ B. Runway incursion avoidance
- ❏ C. Visual scanning and collision avoidance
- ❏ D. Principles of flight
- ❏ E. Airplane flight controls
- ❏ F. Airplane weight and balance
- ❏ G. Navigation and flight planning
- ❏ H. Night operations
- ❏ I. High altitude operations
- ❏ J. 14 CFR and publications
- ❏ K. National airspace system
- ❏ L. Navigation systems and radar services
- ❏ M. Logbook entries and certificate endorsements

III. Preflight Preparation
- ❏ A. Certiflcates and documents
- ❏ B. Weather information
- ❏ C. Operation of systems
- ❏ D. Performance and limitations
- ❏ E. Airworthiness requirements

INDEX